What People Are Saying about Threshold Bible Study

"The distance many feel between the Word of God and their everyday lives can be overwhelming. It need not be so. Threshold Bible Study is a fine blend of the best of biblical scholarship and a realistic sensitivity to the spiritual journey of the believing Christian. I recommend it highly."

■ FRANCIS J. MOLONEY, SDB, *Senior Professorial Fellow*
Australian Catholic University, Melbourne

"Stephen Binz offers an invaluable guide that can make reading the Bible enjoyable and truly nourishing. A real education on how to read the Bible, this series prepares people to discuss Scripture and to share it in community."

■ JACQUES NIEUVIARTS, *Professor of Scripture,*
Institut Catholique de Toulouse, France

"Threshold Bible Study is appropriately named, for its commentary and study questions bring people to the threshold of the text and invite them in. The questions guide but do not dominate. They lead readers to ponder and wrestle with the biblical passages and take them across the threshold toward life with God. Stephen Binz's work stands in the tradition of the biblical renewal movement and brings it back to life. We need more of this in the Church."

■ KATHLEEN M. O'CONNOR, *Professor of Old Testament,*
Columbia Theological Seminary

"I most strongly recommend Stephen Binz's Threshold Bible Study for adult Bible classes, religious education, and personal spiritual enrichment. The series is exceptional for its scholarly solidity, pastoral practicality, and clarity of presentation. The church owes Binz a great debt of gratitude for his generous and competent labor in the service of the Word of God."

■ PETER C. PHAN, *The Ignacio Ellacuria Professor*
of Catholic Social Thought, Georgetown University

"Threshold Bible Study is the perfect series of Bible study books for serious students with limited time. Each lesson is brief, illuminating, challenging, wittily written, and a pleasure to study. The reader will reap a rich harvest of wisdom from the efforts expended."

■ JOHN J. PILCH, *Adjunct Professor of Biblical Studies,*
Georgetown University, Washington, D.C.

"Threshold Bible Study is an enriching and enlightening approach to understanding the rich faith which the Scriptures hold for us today. Written in a clear and concise style, Threshold Bible Study presents solid contemporary biblical scholarship, offers questions for reflection and/or discussion, and then demonstrates a way to pray from the Scriptures. All these elements work together to offer the reader a wonderful insight into how the sacred texts of our faith can touch our lives in a profound and practical way today. I heartily recommend this series to both individuals and to Bible study groups."

■ **ABBOT GREGORY J. POLAN**, OSB,
Conception Abbey and Seminary College

"Threshold Bible Study helpfully introduces the lay reader into the life-enhancing process of Lectio Divina or prayerful reading of Scripture, individually or in a group. This series, prepared by a reputable biblical scholar and teacher, responds creatively to the exhortation of the Council to provide God's people abundant nourishment from the table of God's word. The process proposed leads the reader from Bible study to personal prayer, community involvement, and active Christian commitment in the world."

■ **SANDRA M. SCHNEIDERS**, *Professor of New Testament and Spirituality,*
Jesuit School of Theology, Berkeley

"Stephen Binz has put together a great aid in one of the most important aspects of Catholic Christian life today: Bible study. Largely the purview for non-Catholic Christian laity in the past, recent years have seen Catholics hungering for Scripture study and application in their daily lives. Stephen Binz's series promises to help meet that need."

■ **JOHN MICHAEL TALBOT**, *Catholic Recording Artist,*
Founder of The Brothers and Sisters of Charity
at Little Portion Hermitage

"Threshold Bible Study unlocks the Scriptures and ushers the reader over the threshold into the world of God's living word. The world of the Bible comes alive with new meaning and understanding for our times. This series enables the reader to appreciate contemporary biblical scholarship and the meaning of God's word. This is the best material I have seen for serious Bible study."

■ **MOST REVEREND DONALD W. TRAUTMAN**,
Retired Bishop of Erie

"Threshold Bible Study is that rare kind of program that will help one cross an elusive threshold—using the Bible effectively for prayer and spiritual enrichment. This user-friendly program will enhance any personal or group Bible study. Guaranteed to make your love of Scripture grow!"

■ **RONALD D. WITHERUP**, SS,
Superior General of the Society of St. Sulpice, Paris

THRESHOLD
BIBLE STUDY

CHURCH OF THE HOLY SPIRIT

PART TWO

Acts of the Apostles [15-28]

STEPHEN J. BINZ

TWENTY
THIRD 23rd
PUBLICATIONS
NEW LONDON, CT 06320

TWENTY-THIRD PUBLICATIONS
A Division of Bayard
One Montauk Avenue, Suite 200
New London, CT 06320
(860) 437-3012 or (800) 321-0411
www.23rdpublications.com

The Scripture passages contained herein are from the *New Revised Standard Version Bible*, Catholic edition. Copyright ©1989, by the Division of Christian Education of the National Council of the Churches of Christ in the U.S.A. All rights reserved.

ISBN: 978-1-58595-915-0
Library of Congress Control Number: 2013931009
Printed in the U.S.A.

Contents

LESSONS 13–18

LESSONS 19–24

LESSONS 25–30

How to Use
Threshold Bible Study

T hreshold Bible Study is a dynamic, informative, inspiring, and life-changing series that helps you learn about Scripture in a whole new way. Each book will help you explore new dimensions of faith and discover deeper insights for your life as a disciple of Jesus.

The threshold is a place of transition. The threshold of God's word invites you to enter that place where God's truth, goodness, and beauty can shine into your life and fill your mind and heart. Through the Holy Spirit, the threshold becomes holy ground, sacred space, and graced time. God can teach you best at the threshold, because God opens your life to his word and fills you with the Spirit of truth.

With Threshold Bible Study each topic or book of the Bible is approached in a thematic way. You will understand and reflect on the biblical texts through overarching themes derived from biblical theology. Through this method, the study of Scripture will impact your life in a unique way and transform you from within.

These books are designed for maximum flexibility. Each study is presented in a workbook format, with sections for reading, reflecting, writing, discussing, and praying. Each Threshold book contains thirty lessons, which you can use for your daily study over the course of a month or which can be divided into six lessons per week, providing a group study of six weekly sessions (the first session deals with the Introduction). These studies are ideal for Bible study groups, small Christian communities, adult faith formation, student groups, Sunday school, neighborhood groups, and family reading, as well as for individual learning.

The commentary that follows each biblical passage launches your reflection on that passage and helps you begin to see its significance within the context of your contemporary experience. The questions following the commentary challenge you to understand the passage more fully and apply it to your own life. Space for writing after each question is ideal for personal study and also allows group participants to prepare for the weekly discussion. The prayer helps conclude your study each day by integrating your learning into your relationship with God.

The method of Threshold Bible Study is rooted in the ancient tradition of *lectio divina*, whereby studying the Bible becomes a means of deeper intimacy with God and a transformed life. Reading and interpreting the text (*lectio*) is followed by reflective meditation on its message (*meditatio*). This reading and reflecting flows into prayer from the heart (*oratio* and *contemplatio*). In this way, one listens to God through the Scripture and then responds to God in prayer.

This ancient method assures you that Bible study is a matter of both the mind and the heart. It is not just an intellectual exercise to learn more and be able to discuss the Bible with others. It is, more importantly, a transforming experience. Reflecting on God's word, guided by the Holy Spirit, illumines the mind with wisdom and stirs the heart with zeal.

Following the personal Bible study, Threshold Bible Study offers ways to extend personal *lectio divina* into a weekly conversation with others. This communal experience will allow participants to enhance their appreciation of the message and build up a spiritual community (*collatio*). The end result will be to increase not only individual faith but also faithful witness in the context of daily life (*operatio*).

When bringing Threshold Bible Study to a church community, try to make every effort to include as many people as possible. Many will want to study on their own; others will want to study with family, a group of friends, or a few work associates; some may want to commit themselves to share insights through a weekly conference call, daily text messaging, or an online social network; and others will want to gather weekly in established small groups.

By encouraging Threshold Bible Study and respecting the many ways people desire to make Bible study a regular part of their lives, you will widen the number of people in your church community who study the Bible regularly in whatever way they are able in their busy lives. Simply sign up people at the Sunday services and order bulk quantities for your church. Encourage people to follow the daily study as faithfully as they can. This encouragement can be through Sunday announcements, notices in parish publications, support on the church website, and other creative invitations and motivations.

Through the spiritual disciplines of Scripture reading, study, reflection, conversation, and prayer, Threshold Bible Study will help you experience God's grace more abundantly and root your life more deeply in Christ. The risen Jesus said: "Listen! I am standing at the door, knocking; if you hear my voice and open the door, I will come in to you and eat with you, and you with me" (Rev 3:20). Listen to the Word of God, open the door, and cross the threshold to an unimaginable dwelling with God!

SUGGESTIONS FOR INDIVIDUAL STUDY

• Make your Bible reading a time of prayer. Ask for God's guidance as you read the Scriptures.

• Try to study daily, or as often as possible according to the circumstances of your life.

• Read the Bible passage carefully, trying to understand both its meaning and its personal application as you read. Some persons find it helpful to read the passage aloud.

• Read the passage in another Bible translation. Each version adds to your understanding of the original text.

• Allow the commentary to help you comprehend and apply the scriptural text. The commentary is only a beginning, not the last word, on the meaning of the passage.

• After reflecting on each question, write out your responses. The very act of writing will help you clarify your thoughts, bring new insights, and amplify your understanding.

• As you reflect on your answers, think about how you can live God's word in the context of your daily life.

• Conclude each daily lesson by reading the prayer and continuing with your own prayer from the heart.

• Make sure your reflections and prayers are matters of both the mind and the heart. A true encounter with God's word is always a transforming experience.

• Choose a word or a phrase from the lesson to carry with you throughout the day as a reminder of your encounter with God's life-changing word.

• For additional insights and affirmation, share your learning experience with at least one other person whom you trust. The ideal way to share learning is in a small group that meets regularly.

SUGGESTIONS FOR GROUP STUDY

• Meet regularly; weekly is ideal. Try to be on time, and make attendance a high priority for the sake of the group. The average group meets for about an hour.

• Open each session with a prepared prayer, a song, or a reflection. Find some appropriate way to bring the group from the workaday world into a sacred time of graced sharing.

• If you have not been together before, name tags are very helpful as group members begin to become acquainted with one another.

• Spend the first session getting acquainted with one another, reading the Introduction aloud, and discussing the questions that follow.

• Appoint a group facilitator to provide guidance to the discussion. The role of facilitator may rotate among members each week. The facilitator simply keeps the discussion on track; each person shares responsibility for the group. There is no need for the facilitator to be a trained teacher.

• Try to study the six lessons on your own during the week. When you have done your own reflection and written your own answers, you will be better prepared to discuss the six scriptural lessons with the group. If you have not had an opportunity to study the passages during the week, meet with the group anyway to share support and insights.

• Participate in the discussion as much as you are able, offering your thoughts, insights, feelings, and decisions. You learn by sharing with others the fruits of your study.

• Be careful not to dominate the discussion. It is important that everyone in the group be offered an equal opportunity to share the results of their work. Try to link what you say to the comments of others so that the group remains on the topic.

• When discussing your own personal thoughts or feelings, use "I" language. Be as personal and honest as appropriate, and be very cautious about giving advice to others.

• Listen attentively to the other members of the group so as to learn from their insights. The words of the Bible affect each person in a different way, so a group provides a wealth of understanding for each member.

• Don't fear silence. Silence in a group is as important as silence in personal study. It allows individuals time to listen to the voice of God's Spirit and the opportunity to form their thoughts before they speak.

• Solicit several responses for each question. The thoughts of different people will build on the answers of others and will lead to deeper insights for all.

• Don't fear controversy. Differences of opinions are a sign of a healthy and honest group. If you cannot resolve an issue, continue on, agreeing to disagree. There is probably some truth in each viewpoint.

• Discuss the questions that seem most important for the group. There is no need to cover all the questions in the group session.

• Realize that some questions about the Bible cannot be resolved, even by experts. Don't get stuck on some issue for which there are no clear answers.

• Whatever is said in the group is said in confidence and should be regarded as such.

• Pray as a group in whatever way feels comfortable. Pray for the members of your group throughout the week.

Schedule for Group Study

Session 1: Introduction   Date: _____

Session 2: Lessons 1–6   Date: _____

Session 3: Lessons 7–12   Date: _____

Session 4: Lessons 13–18 Date: _____

Session 5: Lessons 19–24 Date: _____

Session 6: Lessons 25–30 Date: _____

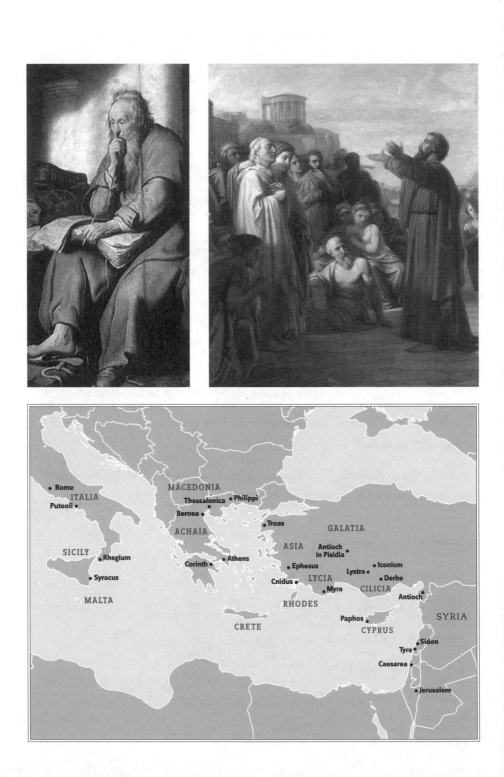

That night the Lord stood near him and said, "Keep up your courage!
For just as you have testified for me in Jerusalem,
so you must bear witness also in Rome." Acts 23:11

Church of the Holy Spirit (Part 2)

The Acts of the Apostles is about the expansion and triumph of the good news of Jesus Christ as it penetrates the world from Jerusalem to Rome. It tells the story of a community of disciples that is centered on God's saving work, led by the Holy Spirit, living faithfully in a way that serves others, and sent to proclaim the gospel through the words and deeds of their lives.

In the first half of Acts, we learned that the shape of the book is formed by the missionary mandate given to the apostles by the risen Lord: "You will be my witnesses in Jerusalem, in all Judea and Samaria, and to the ends of the earth" (1:8). The early episodes demonstrate the growth of the apostolic church in Jerusalem, followed by its expansion to both Jews and Gentiles in the surrounding areas. Then, with the conversion of Paul and his first missionary journey with Barnabas, the church begins to expand to areas of the world outside of Israel.

The second half of Acts starts with the gathering of Peter, James, Paul, and Barnabas, along with the other apostles and elders, at the mother church in Jerusalem. There they encourage and set forth the conditions for the expansion of the gospel to the Gentiles. Then the witness of the apostles to the risen Lord goes forth in earnest into the entire world. Led by Paul, the gospel is preached throughout the provinces of Syria, Galatia, Asia, Macedonia, and Achaia. But Rome, the first-century hub of the world and the imperial capital, is the aim of Paul's missionary travels. While Rome is not itself the "ends of the earth," it is from Rome that the world extends from east to west and from north to south. The goal of Acts, expressed in the Lord's commission that Paul should bear witness in Rome (23:11), expresses the church's ongoing and universal mission to the whole world.

This good news of Jesus Christ, as witnessed by the apostles throughout Acts, is called "the word of God." And throughout Acts, Luke shows us how "the word of God continued to spread and gain adherents" (6:7; 12:24) and how "the word of the Lord grew mightily and prevailed" (19:20). This word of God, as Jesus explained, is like a seed sown that requires good soil to grow. When the word of God is sent forth, people do not always have "ears to hear" or "hearts to receive" the word. But when God's word is heard and heeded, it has the power to save.

As we read and listen to the Acts of the Apostles, we see how the word of God planted in Jerusalem bears a harvest throughout the world. Each harvest creates more seeds, as the word of the Lord grows mightily and prevails in the world. As we study these texts, we must take away whatever obstacles block us from receiving the word in our hearts, so that its saving power will develop within us and so contribute to the growth of the church through the work of God's Spirit.

Reflection and discussion

• What insights did I gain about the gospel and the church from the first half of Acts that will guide me into the second half?

• In what ways is the word of God in Acts and in my own life like seed?

The Holy Spirit Fills the Church from Pentecost to Today

Throughout Acts we increasingly realize that God desires to give his Holy Spirit to all people. In his Pentecost speech Peter quotes from the prophet Joel: "In the last days it will be, God declares, that I will pour out my Spirit upon all flesh." From the time of Pentecost, all the major characters of Acts are filled with the Spirit, enabling them to act and speak with wisdom and courage.

Peter is filled with the Holy Spirit and thus proclaims the message of salvation to the Sanhedrin who have put him on trial (4:8). When Peter and John are released from prison, the entire community of believers receives the Holy Spirit: "When they had prayed, the place in which they were gathered together was shaken; and they were all filled with the Holy Spirit and spoke the word of God with boldness" (4:31). The seven selected to assist the work of the apostles are chosen among those who are "full of the Spirit and of wisdom (6:3). Stephen, in particular, is described as "a man full of faith and the Holy Spirit" (6:5). Stephen speaks with wisdom and the Spirit (6:10), and the gift of the Spirit seems to be most intense at his martyrdom: "Filled with the Holy Spirit, he gazed into heaven and saw the glory of God and Jesus" (7:55). Philip is urged by the Spirit to catch up with the chariot of the Ethiopian and prepare him for baptism; then "the Spirit of the Lord snatched Philip away" to continue his mission (8:29, 39).

Paul receives the Holy Spirit at his initial experience of conversion (9:17), and the Spirit continues to guide his mission throughout the world. The Holy Spirit speaks to the prophets and teachers in the church at Antioch: "Set apart for me Barnabas and Saul for the work to which I have called them" (13:2). As they begin their first journey, which will bring these missionaries to Jews and Gentiles in new lands, they are "sent out by the Holy Spirit" (13:4). The Spirit continues to guide Paul's journeys, even preventing him from going to certain areas of Asia, so that he would be led to journey into Europe for the first time (16:6). The Spirit also leads Paul to make his final and fateful journey up to Jerusalem. In his farewell address at Miletus, Paul says, "Now, as a captive to the Spirit, I am on my way to Jerusalem, not knowing what will happen to me there, except that the Holy Spirit testifies to me in every city that imprisonment and persecution are waiting for me" (20:22-23). The Holy Spirit both warns Paul of suffering and compels him to go. Nothing can stand in the way of God's plan that Paul will witness in the power of the Holy Spirit to the ends of the earth.

By demonstrating to us how all the major figures in Acts are empowered by the Holy Spirit, Luke is showing us that the whole church is guided by the Spirit. This work of the Spirit is shown most explicitly in the watershed event of Acts—the apostolic council in Jerusalem (Acts 15). In that gathering of all the major personalities of Acts, Luke portrays the church reaching a decision through a process of Spirit-guided discernment. Peter testifies that the bestowal of the Holy Spirit on both Jewish and Gentile believers gives evidence that God grants salvation to all in the same way. The decision of the council is expressed as a union of both human and divine action: "It has seemed good to the Holy Spirit and to us." This agreement for the whole church is an interweaving of human discernment and divine guidance in such a way that the decision is a human expression of the divine will. This Jerusalem council has become a model for decision making within the church down through the centuries: a council is called, hears testimony about God's actions among his people, interprets the Scriptures, declares its decisions made in union with the Holy Spirit and the apostolic leaders, and sends out its written teachings to all the local churches scattered throughout the world.

This summary of the testimony of Acts about the work of the Holy Spirit within the church presents a number of conclusions for understanding the role of the Holy Spirit in the church today: 1) The Holy Spirit is the origin and source of life for God's church. 2) We are filled with the Holy Spirit through faith and baptism. 3) As disciples filled with the Holy Spirit, we carry on the work of Jesus in our era. 4) The Holy Spirit empowers us to speak boldly and to act courageously. 5) Because the Holy Spirit fills the lives of believers, Jesus can be present to more people and do more than the limitations of his earthly life allowed. 6) The Holy Spirit guides the church in its mission of evangelization. 7) The mission of the church is universal, crossing every barrier to extend to all people. 8) The Holy Spirit leads us individually to seek out people who are ready for a deeper experience of faith. 9) The Holy Spirit guides the leaders of the church to make decisions that conform to God's will. 10) The Holy Spirit compels us to go places and do things that involve risk and suffering.

Reflection and discussion

• In what ways have I witnessed the Holy Spirit guiding the church during my own lifetime?

• In what ways do I desire to experience the Holy Spirit more actively through my study of Acts?

Paul's Mission to All the Nations

By the end of the first century, Christianity was a worldwide, predominantly Gentile religion due in no small measure to the mission and teachings of Paul. His missionary life demonstrates how Christianity evolved from a messianic movement within Judaism into a worldwide church that embraces believers of every nationality. Although Paul seemed an unlikely candidate for this work, as it turned out, he was just the right person to carry out the expansive ministry entrusted to him. For Paul lived in three cultures: he was a Jew, a Greek, and a Roman—possessing the ideal background for someone who would bring the message of Jesus Christ to the great cities of his day.

First and foremost, Paul was a Jew. He considered himself as belonging to God's chosen people, he was loyal to the Torah, he maintained his Jewish identity in the midst of a pagan world, and he awaited the coming of the kingdom of God, the age to come foretold by Israel's prophets. As a Jew, Paul was a member of a noteworthy and distinctive religion within the vast empire. Grand synagogues could be found in most of the major cities throughout the Mediterranean world. Even after Paul came to believe in Jesus Christ, he always remained a proud member of this ancient faith and understood his mission within the context of its sacred Scriptures.

Paul was also a Greek, and his world was that of Hellenistic culture. Since the days of Alexander the Great, Greek had been the second language and the framework of thought for everyone reached by his conquests. Because Paul was a native of Tarsus, a great center of Greek learning, he not only spoke Greek, but Greek culture, philosophy, and rhetoric enriched his mind and his viewpoint. He read the Scriptures in Greek, the Septuagint version, and so was able to explain the Scriptures in the language of his audience.

Paul was also a Roman citizen, a privilege gained through his family, which he often used to his advantage in his missionary work. In the days of Jesus and Paul, Rome ruled the known world. Paul used the massive system of Roman roads and commerce to travel thousands of miles, establishing churches in cities throughout the Roman world. Yet, Paul was not an uncritical inhabitant of the empire of Caesar. The cult of emperor worship and the massive power of the empire to crush those who tried to interfere with its absolute authority were strong contrasts to the way of Christ. In the face of the imperial propaganda that proclaimed the emperor as savior and lord of the whole world, Paul's gospel message of Christ's lordship was defiantly subversive.

Paul used his international and multicultural experience for the sake of the universal gospel he proclaimed. He was a man who could talk with rabbis on the streets of Jerusalem and with philosophers in the marketplaces of Athens. He knew the ancient wisdom of the Hebrew Scriptures, and he knew the wisdom of Greek literature, such as that of Homer, Sophocles, and Plato. He possessed a Jewish name, Saul, and a Greek and Roman name, Paul.

Paul's divine commission led him to proclaim the gospel by expressing it through the Scriptures and symbols of Israel (the Torah and the temple) and through the language and thought patterns of Greece (philosophy and rhetoric); at the same time he used the communications and transportation systems of Rome to his advantage. He traveled up to the temple in Jerusalem for the feasts of Israel, and he journeyed along the Roman roads to all parts of the world. He knew that the God of Israel was the Creator and Sustainer of the whole world, and therefore he became a man of the whole world in order to bring the very Jewish message of the gospel to all people.

Reflection and discussion

• What might be some of the reasons God chose Paul to bring the gospel to the world?

• How can my understanding of the languages, cultures, and wisdom of the world help make me a better disciple?

Acts is Open-Ended and Unfinished

The way that Luke concludes the book of Acts determines the way that we should read it. The ending is somewhat abrupt, leaving many details untold, but it is presumably the way Luke wanted his narrative to close. It feels quite unfinished because the goal of the work, witnessing to Jesus Christ to the ends of the earth, is incomplete. Luke wants readers to feel the incompleteness of the story and then take up the story in their own lives and continue working toward the goal.

Acts ends with Paul in Rome. After a series of arrests, trials, and escapes, Paul has arrived in Rome and is living under Roman guard. He has appealed his case to the emperor and is awaiting trial. The text's parting words tell us that Paul lives in this situation for two years, preaching with boldness in a manner unhindered. Was Paul ever brought to trial? Was he convicted or released? Was he martyred?

There are many clues in Luke's work suggesting an implied ending for Paul. Paul's story has similar shape to the story of Jesus in Luke's gospel. Both Jesus and Paul are rebuked, arrested, and repeatedly called before leaders to give account of their actions. The lives of both characters are swept up in a relentless journey, Jesus to Jerusalem and Paul to Rome. In Paul's farewell address in Miletus, he tells the elders that he does not count his life as having any value to himself (20:24), and at the end of the speech there is much weeping because Paul had said that he would not see them again (20:38). Paul seems resigned to his own impending death. And since readers know how it ended for Jesus, presumably the end was similar for Paul, as Christian history tells us it was.

But the book of Acts is not really about Paul. Although the second half of the book focuses on him, he remains just one instrument of God's work. The work is about the expansion of the good news of Jesus Christ and the growth of his church, led by the Holy Spirit. Paul's evangelizing ministry in Rome is the zenith of this development, the perfect conclusion of a narrative that repeatedly demonstrates the gospel crossing into new territory. But his work is certainly not the end of the church's witnessing to the ends of the earth. Acts is an unfinished book; it is still being written.

Where are the ends of the earth? From a first-century perspective, Rome is the center of the earth, not its end. For Jews, Greeks, and Romans the world extended far beyond Rome: to Spain and Britain in the west, Scythia in the north, India in the east, and Ethiopia in the south. For the twenty-first-century disciple, the ends of the earth are wherever there are people who have not experienced God's saving love. For you and me, it is all around us.

When Luke wrote his gospel, he knew that the story of Jesus was incomplete, that it must be continued in a second volume. The end of Luke's gospel pointed forward to the story of the church, which he wrote in the Acts of the Apostles. And when he wrote Acts, he knew that the story of the church was incomplete. The evangelizing mission of the church continues. It demands a third volume. Yet, Luke does not write a trilogy; but he implies that it should be written. This third volume is a story that echoes the first two. It is a story similarly empowered and guided by the Holy Spirit. It is a story in which we live out the reality that despite the worst that can happen, God's word progresses, sets people free, transforms lives, and offers salvation.

When we finish our study of Acts, we know that the rest of the story includes all of Luke's readers. We realize that it is the responsibility of each believer to contribute to the evangelizing mission of the church. Luke's ending challenges you and me to press on with the unfinished task.

Reflection and discussion

• Why might Luke not end Acts with the martyrdom of Paul?

• In what ways does Luke's unfinished book inspire and empower me to continue the mission?

Prayer

Lord God, send your Holy Spirit upon me as I continue to listen to your word through the inspired writings of Luke. Prepare my heart to encounter the risen Jesus working through the apostolic ministers of his church. As I continue this study of the Acts of the Apostles, help me to keep changing and growing as I read, reflect, learn, and pray. Stir up within me a passion for the gospel and a desire to evangelize the world around me through the witness of my life. May your word ever increase within me as it continues to expand and triumph in the world.

SUGGESTIONS FOR FACILITATORS, GROUP SESSION 1

1. If the group is meeting for the first time, or if there are newcomers joining the group, it is helpful to provide nametags.

2. Distribute the books to the members of the group.

3. You may want to ask the participants to introduce themselves and tell the group a bit about themselves.

4. Ask one or more of these introductory questions:
   • What drew you to join this group?
   • What is your biggest fear in beginning this Bible study?
   • How is beginning this study like a "threshold" for you?

5. You may want to pray this prayer as a group:

   Come upon us, Holy Spirit, to enlighten and guide us as we continue this study of the Acts of the Apostles. You inspired the writers of the Scriptures to reveal your presence throughout the history of salvation. This inspired word has the power to convert our hearts and change our lives. Fill our hearts with desire, trust, and confidence as you shine the light of your truth within us. Motivate us to read the Scriptures and give us a deeper love for God's word each day. Bless us during this session and throughout the coming week with the fire of your love.

6. Read the Introduction aloud, pausing at each question for discussion. Group members may wish to write the insights of the group as each question is discussed. Encourage several members of the group to respond to each question.

7. Don't feel compelled to finish the complete Introduction during the session. It is better to allow sufficient time to talk about the questions raised than to rush to the end. Group members may read any remaining sections on their own after the group meeting.

8. Instruct group members to read the first six lessons on their own during the six days before the next group meeting. They should write out their own answers to the questions as preparation for next week's group discussion.

9. Fill in the date for each group meeting under "Schedule for Group Study."

10. Conclude the session by praying aloud together the prayer at the end of the Introduction.

"And God, who knows the human heart, testified to them by giving them the Holy Spirit, just as he did to us; and in cleansing their hearts by faith he has made no distinction between them and us." Acts 15:8-9

The Council of the Church in Jerusalem

ACTS 15:1-21 *¹Then certain individuals came down from Judea and were teaching the brothers, "Unless you are circumcised according to the custom of Moses, you cannot be saved." ²And after Paul and Barnabas had no small dissension and debate with them, Paul and Barnabas and some of the others were appointed to go up to Jerusalem to discuss this question with the apostles and the elders. ³So they were sent on their way by the church, and as they passed through both Phoenicia and Samaria, they reported the conversion of the Gentiles, and brought great joy to all the believers. ⁴When they came to Jerusalem, they were welcomed by the church and the apostles and the elders, and they reported all that God had done with them. ⁵But some believers who belonged to the sect of the Pharisees stood up and said, "It is necessary for them to be circumcised and ordered to keep the law of Moses."*

⁶The apostles and the elders met together to consider this matter. ⁷After there had been much debate, Peter stood up and said to them, "My brothers, you know that in the early days God made a choice among you, that I should be the one through whom the Gentiles would hear the message of the good news and become believers. ⁸And God, who knows the human heart, testified to them by giving them the Holy Spirit, just as he did to us; ⁹and in cleansing their hearts by faith he has made no distinction between them and us. ¹⁰Now therefore why are you putting God to the test by placing on the neck of the disciples a yoke that neither our ancestors nor we have been able to bear? ¹¹On the contrary, we believe that we will be saved through the grace of the Lord Jesus, just as they will."

¹²The whole assembly kept silence, and listened to Barnabas and Paul as they told of all the signs and wonders that God had done through them among the Gentiles. ¹³After they finished speaking, James replied, "My brothers, listen to me. ¹⁴Simeon has related how God first looked favorably on the Gentiles, to take from among them a people for his name. ¹⁵This agrees with the words of the prophets, as it is written,

¹⁶ 'After this I will return,
and I will rebuild the dwelling of David, which has fallen;
  from its ruins I will rebuild it,
    and I will set it up,
¹⁷so that all other peoples may seek the Lord—
  even all the Gentiles over whom my name has been called.
  Thus says the Lord, who has been making these things ¹⁸known
    from long ago.'

¹⁹Therefore I have reached the decision that we should not trouble those Gentiles who are turning to God, ²⁰but we should write to them to abstain only from things polluted by idols and from fornication and from whatever has been strangled and from blood. ²¹For in every city, for generations past, Moses has had those who proclaim him, for he has been read aloud every sabbath in the synagogues."

The meeting of Paul and Barnabas with the apostles in Jerusalem gathers all the principal characters of Acts together in what has come to be known as the church's first council. In terms of both its location in the book and its significance for the church, the meeting is central. The church has reached a critical juncture. Ever since Peter's visit to the house of Cornelius, Gentiles have been streaming into the community of disciples. Clearly this was the work of God, fulfilling the divine plan to save all humanity. But, since Jewish Christians understood Jesus as fulfilling the ancient faith of Israel, and since Christianity is a natural extension of Judaism, many of them advocated that Gentiles who become believers should start acting like the people of Israel and fulfill the law of the covenant. This meant circumcision for males, following the Jewish dietary laws, and other practices prescribed in the Torah.

Tension and conflict surrounded this issue in the church's early years, and Luke has summarized a complex debate. The resolution of this matter—whether or not Gentiles need to become Jews to experience salvation through Jesus—is left to the deliberation of the apostles and the guidance of the Holy Spirit. The decision is too important to be left to each local church. A definitive and church-wide resolution of this issue is essential for the church's ongoing mission. On the one hand, many of the Jewish Christian leaders held that, if any part of the Torah should be followed by everyone, it should be circumcision, the sign of the covenant that reaches back to Abraham. Paul and Barnabas, on the other hand, held that salvation in Christ and inclusion in his church comes with the response of faith through the gracious work of Christ.

In his last appearance in Acts, Peter stands up and reviews his own experience as the first to preach the gospel to the Gentiles and call them to faith. He stresses that God's gift of the Spirit was given to them just as it had been given to the Jewish believers at Pentecost. God accepted them just as they were, without any circumcision or works of the law. Peter's conclusion states the principle at the heart of the council's pronouncement: both Jews and Gentiles "will be saved through the grace of the Lord Jesus" (verse 11). Salvation is a gift from God, available equally to both Jews and Gentiles. And since it is God who gives the gift to anyone who responds in faith, the church should put no unnecessary obstacles in the way to salvation.

In a remarkable display of unity, James defends the position expressed by Barnabas and Paul, as well as the position of Peter, whom he refers to using his Jewish name, Simeon. He appeals to Scripture to demonstrate how the Torah and the prophets are fulfilled as the covenant promises are extended to all people. He quotes from the prophet Amos to show that the restored kingdom of Israel will include people of all nations, "so that all other peoples may seek the Lord—even all the Gentiles" (verse 17). Finally, James proposes a practical solution: the Gentile converts were to follow four minimal rules to avoid those things that were particularly offensive to Jews (verse 20). This would allow the Jewish Christians to share meals with the Gentile converts and live in peace with them.

By completely legitimizing the mission to the Gentiles and their full inclusion in the church, the council in Jerusalem forms the firm foundation for the work narrated in the second half of Acts. From here on, the primary action of the book is the gospel going out to the ends of the earth through the work of Paul. This episode from the early church demonstrates the working of the Holy Spirit in a momentous time of decision for the apostles. It shows that the work of the Holy Spirit is both conservative, safeguarding the teachings of Jesus and the ancient Scriptures, and progressive, bringing new understanding in every age of history.

Reflection and discussion

• In what sense is this council of the church in Jerusalem the central event in the Acts of the Apostles?

• Is the decision of the council a victory for one side over another? Is it conservative or progressive?

• The Acts of the Apostles indicates that the early church was never free of tensions and that debate was an important element in communal discernment. What lessons can I learn from the apostles about solving problems and resolving disputes peacefully?

• By leading the church of the first century to accept Gentiles into its fellowship, the Holy Spirit moved the community to become a global church. How does the Holy Spirit lead the church of the twenty-first century to continue this process?

• Why is Peter's insight about God's inclusive grace so critical for the mission of the church? What are its implications for my own discipleship?

Prayer

God of the covenant, I believe that you offer salvation to all the peoples of the earth through the grace of the Lord Jesus. Pour forth your Holy Spirit into my heart, and give me a passion for the gospel and for the mission of your church.

When they gathered the congregation together, they delivered the letter. When its members read it, they rejoiced at the exhortation. Acts 15:30-31

The Council's Letter to Gentile Believers

ACTS 15:22-35 *22Then the apostles and the elders, with the consent of the whole church, decided to choose men from among their members and to send them to Antioch with Paul and Barnabas. They sent Judas called Barsabbas, and Silas, leaders among the brothers, 23with the following letter: "The brothers, both the apostles and the elders, to the believers of Gentile origin in Antioch and Syria and Cilicia, greetings. 24Since we have heard that certain persons who have gone out from us, though with no instructions from us, have said things to disturb you and have unsettled your minds, 25we have decided unanimously to choose representatives and send them to you, along with our beloved Barnabas and Paul, 26who have risked their lives for the sake of our Lord Jesus Christ. 27We have therefore sent Judas and Silas, who themselves will tell you the same things by word of mouth. 28For it has seemed good to the Holy Spirit and to us to impose on you no further burden than these essentials: 29that you abstain from what has been sacrificed to idols and from blood and from what is strangled and from fornication. If you keep yourselves from these, you will do well. Farewell."*

30So they were sent off and went down to Antioch. When they gathered the congregation together, they delivered the letter. 31When its members read it, they rejoiced at the exhortation. 32Judas and Silas, who were themselves prophets, said much to encourage and strengthen the believers. ³³After they had been there for some time, they were sent off in peace by the believers to those who had sent them. ³⁵But Paul and Barnabas remained in Antioch, and there, with many others, they taught and proclaimed the word of the Lord.

After the apostles and elders at the Jerusalem council reach an agreement, they send an apostolic letter along with their own representatives to the Gentiles churches being served by Paul and Barnabas. The letter repeats the decision of the council that Gentiles do not need to become Jews and observe the Torah, except in four matters. These exceptions would allow observant Jewish converts to share table fellowship with the new Gentile Christians.

The letter outlines the problem that led to the council's decision. Certain persons from the community in Jerusalem had overstepped their authority and disturbed the Gentile communities associated with the church in Antioch. The apostles and elders make it clear that the Jewish Christians, who demanded that the Gentiles be circumcised and follow the regulations of the Torah, were not acting under their instruction (verse 24). The letter also states that the church in Jerusalem has sent two men, Judas Barsabbas and Silas, to act as the community's representatives to the newer Gentile churches. Along with Barnabas and Paul, whom the apostles and elders commend as "beloved" ones "who have risked their lives for the sake of our Lord Jesus Christ," these representatives are to personally explain the decision of the council (verses 25-27).

By prefacing their letter with a statement that the church's decision is a result of the apostles' discernment and the affirmation of the Holy Spirit (verse 28), the leaders acknowledge how the gift of the Spirit is alive in the church. They assert the primacy of God's Spirit in guiding and governing the Christian movement. Since the Gentiles are already receiving the Spirit, the issue of Gentile inclusion and salvation has been effectively solved. The work of the Holy Spirit is conserving the essentials of Jesus' teachings and example and also leading the church into a future directed beyond Israel to the whole world.

When the delegation arrives in Antioch, they share the letter with the congregation by reading it aloud, bringing much joy among the Gentile believers.

Judas and Silas exhort the church and bring strength to the congregation there. Then, after staying in Antioch for some time, they were sent back to Jerusalem with a commendation of peace. But Paul and Barnabas remain in Antioch, teaching and proclaiming "the word of the Lord."

This first council enables us to see the process by which the church would continue to decide important issues throughout its history. Reaching a decision is a process of discernment in which debate and conflict are often necessary. The leaders of the church speak after the discussion, and a consensus is reached with the consent of the whole church and decreed under the guidance of the Holy Spirit. The results do not lead to a monochromatic church in which everyone thinks and acts in the same way. Rather, the Jewish believers continue their own practices, but Gentile believers are not forced to live like the Jews. While the church insisted on unity in essential matters, it encouraged diversity and the embodiment of the faith in a variety of cultures.

Reflection and discussion

• Rather than a democratic process, the apostles called their decree the decision of "what seemed good to the Holy Spirit and to us." What are some of the principles involved in this apostolic decision making?

• The decisions of the church today are not just the results of wise compromise or effective strategic planning. How does the Holy Spirit continue to guide the church today?

• What are some of the differences between the primarily Jewish church in Jerusalem and the primarily Gentile church in Antioch?

• What are some of the elements of unity between the church in Jerusalem and the church in Antioch?

• What can the worldwide church today learn from the relationship between the church in Jerusalem and in Antioch?

Prayer

Holy Spirit, continue to guide the church today as you directed the apostles and elders in Jerusalem. Through debate and discernment, direct the leaders of our church toward decisions that express your will, and help them to revere the cultural diversity of the worldwide church.

As they went from town to town, they delivered to them for observance the decisions that had been reached by the apostles and elders who were in Jerusalem. Acts 16:4

Paul Travels with Silas and Timothy

ACTS 15:36–16:5 *³⁶After some days Paul said to Barnabas, "Come, let us return and visit the believers in every city where we proclaimed the word of the Lord and see how they are doing." ³⁷Barnabas wanted to take with them John called Mark. ³⁸But Paul decided not to take with them one who had deserted them in Pamphylia and had not accompanied them in the work. ³⁹The disagreement became so sharp that they parted company; Barnabas took Mark with him and sailed away to Cyprus. ⁴⁰But Paul chose Silas and set out, the believers commending him to the grace of the Lord. ⁴¹He went through Syria and Cilicia, strengthening the churches.*

16 ¹Paul went on also to Derbe and to Lystra, where there was a disciple named Timothy, the son of a Jewish woman who was a believer; but his father was a Greek. ²He was well spoken of by the believers in Lystra and Iconium. ³Paul wanted Timothy to accompany him; and he took him and had him circumcised because of the Jews who were in those places, for they all knew that his father was a Greek. ⁴As they went from town to town, they delivered to them for observance the decisions that had been reached by the apostles and elders who were in Jerusalem. ⁵So the churches were strengthened in the faith and increased in numbers daily.

From Antioch Paul expresses his desire to return to all the churches he has established and in which he has proclaimed "the word of the Lord." He wants to follow up on his earlier efforts and see how the communities are flourishing. Paul proposes that Barnabas join him, but a dispute arises over whether to take John Mark along. Barnabas wishes to bring him, since the young man is his cousin (Col 4:10), but Paul does not wish to bring John Mark because of his withdrawal from them on their first mission. Paul is probably concerned about whether the youthful John Mark will persevere in the rigors and trials of the journey. The disagreement of Paul and Barnabas results in two separate missions instead of one: Barnabas takes John Mark with him and travels to Cyprus, while Paul takes Silas with him. From here on, Acts follows the travels of Paul exclusively.

Paul begins his second recorded journey of Acts, traveling first through Syria and Cilicia. After strengthening the churches in those regions, he returns to Derbe and then to Lystra. There Paul discovers Timothy, a disciple highly regarded by the believers of the region. Paul desires Timothy to accompany him as he continues his journey.

Timothy, however, has not been circumcised, although he is the son of a Jewish believer, Eunice, and the grandson of another Jewish believer, Lois (2 Tim 1:5). Although his father is Gentile, marriages of mixed religions were forbidden in Judaism, but when they occurred, children were to be raised as Jews. In addition, an uncircumcised son of a Jewish mother was regarded in Judaism as a violator of the covenant. So Paul's dilemma regarding Timothy concerned his credibility among the Jews among whom they would travel and minister.

Paul's solution is to have Timothy circumcised out of sensitivity and respect for Jewish religious concerns. Circumcision will ensure Timothy's credibility and ensure that debate over Timothy's lineage does not overshadow the message of the gospel. As Paul, Silas, and Timothy travel together, they deliver to the churches in each place "the decisions that had been reached by the apostles and elders who were in Jerusalem." Paul's decision regarding Timothy's circumcision is in line with the sensitivity to both the Jewish and Gentile culture recommended by the Jewish council. Because of this cultural concern and the zeal of these missionaries, the churches are strengthened and they continue to grow.

Reflection and discussion

• The solution reached by Paul and Barnabas to their disagreement recognized the need for separate ministries. How did their compromise allow the advance of the gospel to continue?

• What seem to be some of the differences between Paul and Barnabas in terms of their personalities and missionary styles?

• How do leaders in the church discern which issues are central to the gospel and worth standing up for and which are not worth elevating to an importance they do not deserve?

Prayer

Risen Lord, since you called the apostles Paul and Barnabas to proclaim the gospel, their commitment to their mission surpassed the obstacles of their disagreement and separation from each other. Give me a passionate love for those to whom I am sent by you.

When he had seen the vision, we immediately tried to cross over
to Macedonia, being convinced that God had called us
to proclaim the good news to them. Acts 16:10

Crossing from Asia to Europe

ACTS 16:6-15 *⁶They went through the region of Phrygia and Galatia, having been forbidden by the Holy Spirit to speak the word in Asia. ⁷When they had come opposite Mysia, they attempted to go into Bithynia, but the Spirit of Jesus did not allow them; ⁸so, passing by Mysia, they went down to Troas. ⁹During the night Paul had a vision: there stood a man of Macedonia pleading with him and saying, "Come over to Macedonia and help us." ¹⁰When he had seen the vision, we immediately tried to cross over to Macedonia, being convinced that God had called us to proclaim the good news to them.*

¹¹We set sail from Troas and took a straight course to Samothrace, the following day to Neapolis, ¹²and from there to Philippi, which is a leading city of the district of Macedonia and a Roman colony. We remained in this city for some days. ¹³On the sabbath day we went outside the gate by the river, where we supposed there was a place of prayer; and we sat down and spoke to the women who had gathered there. ¹⁴A certain woman named Lydia, a worshiper of God, was listening to us; she was from the city of Thyatira and a dealer in purple cloth.

The Lord opened her heart to listen eagerly to what was said by Paul. [15]When she and her household were baptized, she urged us, saying, "If you have judged me to be faithful to the Lord, come and stay at my home." And she prevailed upon us.

Luke makes it clear that the further advancement of the gospel is directed by the Holy Spirit. As in the case of Peter's movement to the Gentiles and Philip's encounter with the Ethiopian, Paul's westward outreach is guided by the Spirit. In narrating the spread of the gospel from Jerusalem to Rome, the first momentous step is Paul's crossing from Asia to Europe. In today's geography this is a crossing from Turkey to Greece.

When the Spirit prevents Paul from carrying out his own plans, a vision urges him to proceed into Europe (verse 9). Paul and his companions are in Troas, located on the northwest tip of Asia Minor, near ancient Troy. In Paul's vision, a man from Macedonia pleads with Paul, asking him to cross over into Macedonia to help them. Immediately Paul makes plans for the crossing, convinced that God has called him to bring the message of salvation to them. Very few of Paul's missionary encounters ever turned out as Paul would have imagined, yet God's plan produces wonderful results.

Here begin the so-called "we" passages, in which the narrator switches from third person to first person. The traditional explanation for this sudden shift from "they" to "we" is that Luke himself accompanies Paul on these parts of his journeys. Others explain that the shift of person is due to Luke's use of a different source for this material. However, using first-person sources from someone else and not identifying them as eyewitnesses seems improbable. After this section, the "we" passages are found in 20:5-15, 21:1-18, and 27:1–28:16.

After sailing to the island of Samothrace, Paul and his company make their way to Neapolis, a port city of Macedonia. After traveling ten more miles, they reach Philippi, a wealthy city and Roman colony. Arriving on the Sabbath, Paul thinks he will find a house of prayer—a synagogue where men would be gathered. Instead, he enters into conversation with a group of women who have gathered outside the city gates by the river (verse 13). The location allows for ceremonial washings as well as prayer.

Among the women, there is one named Lydia, whose occupation as a dealer in purple goods implies that she is a woman of some wealth. She is also described as "a worshiper of God," a term that often describes a former polytheist who becomes a worshiper of the God of Israel and attends the synagogue. God opens her heart to listen to and accept the message of Paul. Lydia's belief leads to the baptism of her and her household, making her the first of a long history of Christian conversions in Europe (verse 15). She expresses her gratitude by opening her house as the first house church and missionary base in Europe.

Reflection and discussion

• How does the closed door of verse 7 lead to another open door for the gospel? What examples from my life show how God works through life's unexpected circumstances? Am I able to trust my future to God when I cannot see it clearly?

• In describing Lydia's conversion, Luke says, "The Lord opened her heart to listen eagerly to what was said by Paul." What are some of the ways that God continues to open hearts today?

Prayer

Most High God, your ways are not my ways. When things don't go my way, teach me to trust that you have a better plan. Thank you for surprising me with unexpected blessings.

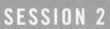
The crowd joined in attacking them, and the magistrates had them stripped of their clothing and ordered them to be beaten with rods. Acts 16:22

Paul and Silas Beaten and Imprisoned in Philippi

ACTS 16:16-24 *¹⁶One day, as we were going to the place of prayer, we met a slave girl who had a spirit of divination and brought her owners a great deal of money by fortune-telling. ¹⁷While she followed Paul and us, she would cry out, "These men are slaves of the Most High God, who proclaim to you a way of salvation." ¹⁸She kept doing this for many days. But Paul, very much annoyed, turned and said to the spirit, "I order you in the name of Jesus Christ to come out of her." And it came out that very hour.*

¹⁹But when her owners saw that their hope of making money was gone, they seized Paul and Silas and dragged them into the marketplace before the authorities. ²⁰When they had brought them before the magistrates, they said, "These men are disturbing our city; they are Jews ²¹and are advocating customs that are not lawful for us as Romans to adopt or observe." ²²The crowd joined in attacking them, and the magistrates had them stripped of their clothing and ordered them to be beaten with rods. ²³After they had given them a severe flogging, they threw them into prison and ordered the jailer to keep them securely. ²⁴Following these instructions, he put them in the innermost cell and fastened their feet in the stocks.

While in Philippi, Paul encounters a slave girl who has "a spirit of divination," literally, a Pythonian spirit. Python is a reference to the soothsaying divinity, originally conceived of as a snake or dragon that inhabited Delphi. After Python was slain by the god Apollo, the spirit inhabited beautiful girls and wise crones, allowing them to foretell the future. Because soothsaying was a profitable religious art, this slave girl was bringing a great deal of income to her owners.

The girl followed Paul and his companions for many days, uttering the truth about Paul and his company—"These men are slaves of the Most High God, who proclaim to you a way of salvation" (verse 17)—just as the demonic spirits in the gospel recognized the truth about Jesus (Luke 4:34; 8:28). While her utterance is ironically true, it may also be misleading. She could be understood as saying that Paul's God is the highest among many gods, offering one among many ways to salvation. So, when Paul becomes disturbed by her declarations, he moves to stop her by showing his power over such forces (verse 18). Speaking in the name of Jesus Christ, Paul expels the spirit and it immediately comes out of her.

Paul's action is not well received by the girl's owners, who are earning money from her activity. Their income is more important to them than her dignity or salvation. So they seize Paul and bring him to the marketplace where, as in most Roman cities, there is a raised judgment seat on which the magistrates sit to render decisions.

They complain that if the citizens are encouraged to become Christians, their new loyalties will direct them away from fidelity to the emperor and the myriad religions of Rome. The owners also complain that if this new religion is adopted, with acts similar to the one Paul performed, the city would lose the commerce involved with the Roman deities and anyone could be at risk of losing their livelihood. This charge of "disturbing our city" is what the officials cannot allow.

Paul and his company have no opportunity to defend themselves against the charges. The judgment is followed by an attack from the crowd and the order from the magistrates that they be beaten with rods in public. After the beating, they are thrown into the prison and fastened with chains and stocks. The magistrates plan to hold them for a time in order to make an example of them and to discourage them from continuing to preach.

Reflection and discussion

• Why was Paul annoyed at the utterances of the slave girl even though she spoke the truth about him?

• Why did the owners of the slave girl reject the gospel that Paul preached? What is the meaning of their charge against him?

• What financial and economic matters sometimes keep people from following Jesus today?

Prayer

Lord and Master, you free the captive and save the oppressed. Unchain me from the insecurity and greed that prevent me from following your gospel and entrusting my life to you.

Suddenly there was an earthquake, so violent that the foundations
of the prison were shaken; and immediately all the doors were opened
and everyone's chains were unfastened. Acts 16:26

Deliverance of Paul and Silas from Prison

ACTS 16:25-40 *²⁵About midnight Paul and Silas were praying and singing hymns to God, and the prisoners were listening to them. ²⁶Suddenly there was an earthquake, so violent that the foundations of the prison were shaken; and immediately all the doors were opened and everyone's chains were unfastened. ²⁷When the jailer woke up and saw the prison doors wide open, he drew his sword and was about to kill himself, since he supposed that the prisoners had escaped. ²⁸But Paul shouted in a loud voice, "Do not harm yourself, for we are all here." ²⁹The jailer called for lights, and rushing in, he fell down trembling before Paul and Silas. ³⁰Then he brought them outside and said, "Sirs, what must I do to be saved?" ³¹They answered, "Believe on the Lord Jesus, and you will be saved, you and your household." ³²They spoke the word of the Lord to him and to all who were in his house. ³³At the same hour of the night he took them and washed their wounds; then he and his entire family were baptized without delay. ³⁴He brought them up into the house and set food before them; and he and his entire household rejoiced that he had become a believer in God.*

³⁵When morning came, the magistrates sent the police, saying, "Let those men go." ³⁶And the jailer reported the message to Paul, saying, "The magistrates sent word to let you go; therefore come out now and go in peace." [37]But Paul replied, "They have beaten us in public, uncondemned, men who are Roman citizens, and have thrown us into prison; and now are they going to discharge us in secret? Certainly not! Let them come and take us out themselves." [38]The police reported these words to the magistrates, and they were afraid when they heard that they were Roman citizens; [39]so they came and apologized to them. And they took them out and asked them to leave the city. [40]After leaving the prison they went to Lydia's home; and when they had seen and encouraged the brothers and sisters there, they departed.

Paul and Silas continue to make the best of unexpected circumstances as they pray and sing hymns in their cell while the other prisoners listen. When an earthquake shakes the prison, the doors are all opened and the fetters are unfastened. Although earthquakes are common in Macedonia, the timing and results of the quake point to the action of God, showing that the liberation of the prisoners is the work of divine providence. The jailer seeks to take his own life, assuming that he would be severely punished for allowing the prisoners to escape under his watch. But Paul stops him by shouting that all the prisoners are still present in the jail.

All of these events—the earthquake, their singing and praying in prison, their calm amidst the earthquake, and the words of the servant girl about them—convince the jailer that Paul and Silas are indeed "slaves of the Most High God," bringing to him a way of salvation (verse 17). He immediately rushes in and falls trembling before Paul and Silas, asking them, "What must I do to be saved?" (verse 30). Paul explains that faith in the Lord Jesus is the way to salvation for the jailer and his household. Paul and his companions then offer fuller instructions to them about Jesus and his lordship, speaking to them "the word of the Lord." After the jailer washes the wounds of Paul and Silas, the missionaries "wash" the jailer and his household and claim them for Jesus Christ in the waters of baptism (verse 33). Filled with the joy of salvation, the household share a meal with Paul and his company, possibly including a eucharistic celebration.

When the magistrates hear about the events, they order that Paul and Silas be let go. But, at this point, Paul reveals that he and Silas are Roman citizens, a people whom Roman law forbids from being beaten. The missionaries refuse to simply leave quietly, charging the magistrates with beating and jailing them without trial, which are violations of their rights as Roman citizens (verse 37). Paul has not previously mentioned his Roman citizenship because he does not want to dilute his public witness. He wants his audience to know that his loyalty is to Jesus Christ, before any allegiance to the empire. In addition, he wishes to emphasize the injustice of persecution for the faith. If he escapes suffering due to his status as a Roman citizen, he avoids his solidarity with the Christians of Philippi in being willing to share in the sufferings of Christ.

Paul wishes to make his innocence a matter of public record and to be publicly escorted out of the prison. At the least, Paul and Silas are owed an apology by the magistrates. So the officials come to the jail, apologize to the men, and ask them to leave the city to assure its peace. Their public release added extra security for the Christians of Philippi, assuring that the magistrates will be more careful in the future. Paul and Silas graciously agree to leave the city, but first they go to the house of Lydia to visit and encourage the believers there.

Throughout his time in Philippi, Paul's ministry is summarized by his engagement with the central character of each scene: Lydia, the wealthy dealer in purple goods; the slave girl, oppressed by her owners for their own profits; and the jailer, a Gentile bureaucrat of the Roman government. Together they express the scope of Paul's ministry and the transforming power of the gospel. God's liberating grace is effective in the lives of everyone, in all of their social, economic, ethnic, and psychological diversity.

Reflection and discussion

• In what way does the divine release of Paul and Silas from prison express the redemption of the jailer? How does the episode challenge the reader to consider who is truly free?

• Why has Paul been reluctant to reveal his Roman citizenship until this event? How did Paul claim his citizenship in a way that was beneficial to his fellow believers?

• In what ways might the singing and praying of Paul and Silas in prison be a Christian witness to the jailer and the other prisoners? How can the gospel affect prisoners and those involved in the prison system today?

• In his letter to the Philippians, written to the community some years after these events, Paul speaks about knowing peace and joy in the midst of hardships. How might these experiences in Philippi have influenced his words in Philippians 4:4-7, 12-13?

Prayer

Lord Jesus, whether I am well fed or hungry, satisfied or distressed, you offer me contentment in all circumstances. I can do all things and rejoice always because you are the source of my strength and my peace.

SUGGESTIONS FOR FACILITATORS, GROUP SESSION 2

1. If there are newcomers who were not present for the first group session, introduce them now.

2. You may want to pray this prayer as a group:

Most High God, through the ministry of Paul, Barnabas, John Mark, Timothy, and Silas, you have given us a zeal for the gospel and a desire to evangelize. Pour forth your Holy Spirit upon us so that we may participate in the mission of your church. Teach us to trust in your plan so that we may find your blessings in unexpected places and circumstances. Through our words and actions, open the hearts of people so that your grace may fill their hearts. Help us to believe that we can do all things and rejoice always because you are the source of our strength and our peace.

3. Ask one or more of the following questions:
   - What was your biggest challenge in Bible study over this past week?
   - What did you learn about yourself this week?

4. Discuss together lessons 1 through 6. Assuming that group members have read the Scripture and commentary during the week, there is no need to read it aloud. As you review each lesson, you might want to briefly summarize the Scripture passages of each lesson and ask the group what stands out most clearly from the commentary.

5. Choose one or more of the questions for reflection and discussion from each lesson to talk over as a group. You may want to ask group members which question was most challenging or helpful to them as you review each lesson.

6. Keep the discussion moving, but don't rush the discussion in order to complete more questions. Allow time for the questions that provoke the most discussion.

7. Instruct group members to complete lessons 7 through 12 on their own during the six days before the next group meeting. They should write out their own answers to the questions as preparation for next week's group discussion.

8. Conclude by praying aloud together the prayer at the end of lesson 6, or any other prayer you choose.

But the Jews became jealous, and with the help of some ruffians in the marketplaces they formed a mob and set the city in an uproar. Acts 17:5

Uproar in Thessalonica and Beroea

ACTS 17:1-15 *¹After Paul and Silas had passed through Amphipolis and Apollonia, they came to Thessalonica, where there was a synagogue of the Jews. ²And Paul went in, as was his custom, and on three sabbath days argued with them from the scriptures, ³explaining and proving that it was necessary for the Messiah to suffer and to rise from the dead, and saying, "This is the Messiah, Jesus whom I am proclaiming to you." ⁴Some of them were persuaded and joined Paul and Silas, as did a great many of the devout Greeks and not a few of the leading women. ⁵But the Jews became jealous, and with the help of some ruffians in the marketplaces they formed a mob and set the city in an uproar. While they were searching for Paul and Silas to bring them out to the assembly, they attacked Jason's house. ⁶When they could not find them, they dragged Jason and some believers before the city authorities, shouting, "These people who have been turning the world upside down have come here also, ⁷and Jason has entertained them as guests. They are all acting contrary to the decrees of the emperor, saying that there is another king named Jesus." ⁸The people and the city officials were disturbed when they heard this, ⁹and after they had taken bail from Jason and the others, they let them go.*

¹⁰That very night the believers sent Paul and Silas off to Beroea; and when they arrived, they went to the Jewish synagogue. ¹¹These Jews were more receptive than those in Thessalonica, for they welcomed the message very eagerly and examined the scriptures every day to see whether these things were so. ¹²Many of them therefore believed, including not a few Greek women and men of high standing. ¹³But when the Jews of Thessalonica learned that the word of God had been proclaimed by Paul in Beroea as well, they came there too, to stir up and incite the crowds. ¹⁴Then the believers immediately sent Paul away to the coast, but Silas and Timothy remained behind. ¹⁵Those who conducted Paul brought him as far as Athens; and after receiving instructions to have Silas and Timothy join him as soon as possible, they left him.

Paul's mission to the Gentiles was never in any way an abandonment of his commitment to Judaism. In both Thessalonica and Beroea, he is very much a Jewish preacher, teaching from the Scriptures of Israel and demonstrating that Jesus is the Messiah. In each place, the response to the good news is mixed, as many Jews as well as Greek women and men are persuaded by Paul, but many also reject his preaching. The jury of the world is still out on the new faith.

Traveling westward along the famous Via Egnatia, connecting the eastern and western parts of the Roman Empire, Paul and Silas arrive at Thessalonica, a large metropolis of Macedonia. As was Paul's custom when arriving in major cities, he goes first to the synagogue. There he presents the case for Jesus from the ancient Scriptures at three assemblies on the Sabbath.

His case is described as "explaining and proving" that God is at work through Jesus (verse 3). First, Paul demonstrates that the Scriptures foretold that the Messiah would suffer and rise from the dead. Then, he shows that Jesus is the Messiah, the redeemer of Israel for whom the people have been waiting.

Paul's presentations persuade some of the Jews and they become part of the Christian community. His greater success, however, seems to be among the Gentiles: "a great many of the devout Greeks and not a few of the leading women" (verse 4). So those who respond favorable to Paul include both Jews and Gentiles, men and women, and all the social classes. But there is also opposition to Paul. Some in the Jewish community find his message a threat, so they gather a mob from some of the ruffians in the marketplace.

The rabble attacks the house of a man named Jason, who is the host for the missionaries. It seems that many of the new Christians in Thessalonica are gathering at his home for worship and fellowship. When the mob is unable to find Paul and Silas, they drag Jason and some of the other believers to a hearing before the city officials.

Because of the skirmish, the accusers shout out the charges against Paul and Silas to the authorities. They allege that the missionaries have been "turning the world upside down," a claim that they are upsetting the established order of things throughout the empire. The adversaries of Paul and Silas charge that these revolutionaries have come to do the same in Thessalonica. They also accuse the missionaries of "acting contrary to the decrees of the emperor," saying that Jesus is another king.

This charge of sedition, trying to overthrow the emperor, is the charge also brought against Jesus at his trial (Luke 23:2). Those in charge of the city have a duty to put down sedition and to make sure that the emperor's place is not challenged. Of course, neither Jesus nor the early missionaries of the church sought to overthrow the emperor, but the influence of the Christian movement is clearly provoking rumors to that effect.

The city officials do not seem convinced by the evidence, but they take bail from Jason and other believers as assurance they will not break the Roman law. The believers send Paul and Silas from the city in order to keep peace in the city and to keep the missionaries safe. Paul's letters to the Thessalonians indicate, however, that the persecution of the Christians there continued (1 Thess 3:1-5).

When Paul arrives in Beroea, he finds a much more receptive audience in the synagogue there (verse 11). They eagerly welcome the gospel message and study the Scriptures daily, and many become believers. As in Thessalonica, a mixed audience receives the message, including both Jews and Greeks as well as women and men of all social classes. But the opponents from Thessalonica catch up with them and stir up the people of Beroea. Again, the Christians send Paul away, leaving Silas and Timothy behind until Paul will send for them.

Reflection and discussion

• Over and over Paul is forced to move on to new locations after preaching the gospel. Why is the message he preaches so threatening and divisive?

• Paul and his companions are charged with "turning the world upside down" as they proclaim the good news throughout the Roman Empire. In what sense is this accusation false and in what sense is it true?

• When has my belief in Jesus Christ led to conflicts with other authorities who claim my allegiance?

Prayer

Lord Jesus, you alone are king and lord of the world, and you reign over my life. As I seek to follow the gospel and study the Scriptures, teach me how to evangelize and bring others closer to you.

"As I went through the city and looked carefully at the objects
of your worship, I found among them an altar with the inscription,
'To an unknown god.' What therefore you worship as unknown,
this I proclaim to you." Acts 17:23

Paul Evangelizes
the Athenians

ACTS 17:16-34 ¹⁶*While Paul was waiting for them in Athens, he was deeply distressed to see that the city was full of idols. ¹⁷So he argued in the synagogue with the Jews and the devout persons, and also in the marketplace every day with those who happened to be there. ¹⁸Also some Epicurean and Stoic philosophers debated with him. Some said, "What does this babbler want to say?" Others said, "He seems to be a proclaimer of foreign divinities." (This was because he was telling the good news about Jesus and the resurrection.) ¹⁹So they took him and brought him to the Areopagus and asked him, "May we know what this new teaching is that you are presenting? ²⁰It sounds rather strange to us, so we would like to know what it means." ²¹Now all the Athenians and the foreigners living there would spend their time in nothing but telling or hearing something new.*

²²Then Paul stood in front of the Areopagus and said, "Athenians, I see how extremely religious you are in every way. ²³For as I went through the city and looked carefully at the objects of your worship, I found among them an altar with the inscription, 'To an unknown god.' What therefore you worship as unknown, this I proclaim to you. ²⁴The God who made the world and everything in it, he who is Lord of heaven and earth, does not live in shrines made by human hands, ²⁵nor is he served by human hands, as though he needed anything, since he himself gives to all mortals life and breath and all things. ²⁶From one ancestor he made all nations to inhabit the whole earth, and he allotted the times of their existence and the boundaries of the places where they would live, ²⁷so that they would search for God and perhaps grope for him and find him— though indeed he is not far from each one of us. ²⁸For 'In him we live and move and have our being'; as even some of your own poets have said,

'For we too are his offspring.'

²⁹Since we are God's offspring, we ought not to think that the deity is like gold, or silver, or stone, an image formed by the art and imagination of mortals. ³⁰While God has overlooked the times of human ignorance, now he commands all people everywhere to repent, ³¹because he has fixed a day on which he will have the world judged in righteousness by a man whom he has appointed, and of this he has given assurance to all by raising him from the dead."

³²When they heard of the resurrection of the dead, some scoffed; but others said, "We will hear you again about this." ³³At that point Paul left them. ³⁴But some of them joined him and became believers, including Dionysius the Areopagite and a woman named Damaris, and others with them.

Although the golden age of Athens had passed, the city was still considered the intellectual capital of the Greco-Roman world in the days of Paul. Athens represented the philosophy and culture of ancient Greece and was filled with fine examples of art and architecture. As Paul walks through the Acropolis, the agora, and the streets of the city, he sees the representations of many gods in the temples, in the niches of buildings, and on street corners.

As a monotheistic Jew, Paul sees these not as objects of art but as idolatry, and he is deeply distressed by them. In this cosmopolitan city, Paul would have encountered a wide diversity of people, from the Jews who met in the synagogue to the variety of people from many nations whom he encountered in the marketplace (verse 17). As he contends with audiences, his message is misunderstood. Some of the philosophers accuse him of being a "babbler," literally, one who picks up bits of news as a bird pecks at seeds. They also accuse him of being "a proclaimer of foreign divinities," perhaps because he speaks of Jesus and resurrection (verse 18), which sounds to his hearers like a pair of new gods (in Greek, *Iesous* and *Anastasis*).

The philosophers and people of Athens bring Paul to the Areopagus, known in Latin as Mars Hill. Here Athenians gather to hear matters of legal, political, and religious significance. Asked to explain his new teaching, Paul fashions his response in a well-constructed piece of classical rhetoric. He does not condemn Greek teachings in order to replace them with the gospel. Instead, he argued that all people are groping for the truth about God.

This search for truth—expressed in shrines and statues, poetry and philosophy—is a proper foundation for the revelation of the one God of all. His notice of an altar "To an unknown god" becomes the springboard for proclaiming "the God who made the world and everything in it, he who is Lord of heaven and earth" (verses 23-24).

The scene presents the most complete example in Acts of how Paul addresses a purely Gentile audience. Rather than base his arguments on the Jewish Scriptures, he forms his discourses from the tenets of Greek philosophy. He offers a model of how Jerusalem can speak to Athens, how divine revelation contained in Scripture can dialogue with the human reason of philosophy. Paul uses Greek writers as legitimate conversation partners in approaching the truth of the gospel. Christian teaching would continue to build on Greek philosophy in future ages: Augustine on Plato and Thomas Aquinas on Aristotle.

Speculative thinking, however, can only move people to the edges of faith. Philosophy can help people understand that divine revelation is reasonable, but it is not enough for belief. Human reason can create the springboard; but faith ultimately requires a leap. The God of all people, about whom Paul speaks, is also the living and personal God revealed in the tradition and Scriptures of Israel. Before this God all people must repent, and in this one God all people must come to believe. The resurrection of Jesus from the dead is humanity's assurance that this God is indeed the Lord of heaven and earth.

Reflection and discussion

• What truths about God did the Greek philosophers and poets express? What words of these Athenian thinkers help me as I seek to grasp the existence of God?

• What are some of the positive signs Paul saw in Athens? What are some of the positive signs in our culture today that express people's searching and longing?

• In what ways can Paul's speech and work in Athens be a model or example of how Christians can dialogue with other religions and the secular world today?

Prayer

God of heaven and earth, you are the one God in whom "we live and move and have our being." Because you have instilled a natural longing for you in the hearts of all people, all people in some way search for you. Help me to trust that you are "not far from each of us."

Crispus, the official of the synagogue, became a believer in the Lord, together with all his household; and many of the Corinthians who heard Paul became believers and were baptized. Acts 18:8

Paul's Ministry in Corinth

ACTS 18:1-17 ¹*After this Paul left Athens and went to Corinth. ²There he found a Jew named Aquila, a native of Pontus, who had recently come from Italy with his wife Priscilla, because Claudius had ordered all Jews to leave Rome. Paul went to see them, ³and, because he was of the same trade, he stayed with them, and they worked together—by trade they were tentmakers. ⁴Every sabbath he would argue in the synagogue and would try to convince Jews and Greeks.*

⁵When Silas and Timothy arrived from Macedonia, Paul was occupied with proclaiming the word, testifying to the Jews that the Messiah was Jesus. ⁶When they opposed and reviled him, in protest he shook the dust from his clothes and said to them, "Your blood be on your own heads! I am innocent. From now on I will go to the Gentiles." ⁷Then he left the synagogue and went to the house of a man named Titius Justus, a worshiper of God; his house was next door to the synagogue. ⁸Crispus, the official of the synagogue, became a believer in the Lord, together with all his household; and many of the Corinthians who heard Paul became believers and were baptized. ⁹One night the Lord said to Paul in a vision, "Do not be afraid, but speak and do not be silent; ¹⁰for I am with you, and no one will lay a hand on you to harm you, for there are many in this city who are my people." ¹¹He stayed there a year and six months, teaching the word of God among them.

¹²But when Gallio was proconsul of Achaia, the Jews made a united attack on Paul and brought him before the tribunal. ¹³They said, "This man is persuading people to worship God in ways that are contrary to the law." ¹⁴Just as Paul was about to speak, Gallio said to the Jews, "If it were a matter of crime or serious villainy, I would be justified in accepting the complaint of you Jews; ¹⁵but since it is a matter of questions about words and names and your own law, see to it yourselves; I do not wish to be a judge of these matters." ¹⁶And he dismissed them from the tribunal. ¹⁷Then all of them seized Sosthenes, the official of the synagogue, and beat him in front of the tribunal. But Gallio paid no attention to any of these things.

As we read Acts, we get a picture of Paul as constantly on the road. Yet, it is important to realize that Luke often condenses a considerable amount of time into just a few verses. We would like to know more about Paul's stay in each place and more about the distinctive qualities of each place. But Luke only gives us selected information—only the developments he considered most important in showing the spread of the faith from Jerusalem to Rome. Although Paul stayed for a year and a half in Corinth, we have only these verses to highlight a few aspects of his work there. Since we have already seen selected episodes of how Paul preached and ministered wherever he went, Luke has no need to repeat himself at each location. Essentially, Paul's long stay in Corinth is summarized in one verse: "He stayed there a year and six months, teaching the word of God among them" (verse 11). Fortunately, we have two letters written by Paul to the Corinthians from which we can glean much about Paul's teaching and the life of the church in Corinth.

Corinth was a large and prosperous city of Greece. With a harbor on each side, to the east and west on the Mediterranean Sea, it was a major city for sea trade. Situated at the junction between the Peloponnesian Peninsula to the south and the mainland to the north, the city was truly a crossroads for travel, commerce, and cultural exchange. As a major port, the city had a reputation for both prosperity and licentiousness. We are able to date the time of Paul's stay to around the years AD 51-52 because those were the years that Gallio was proconsul of Achaia (verse 12).

Here we are first introduced to Aquila and Priscilla, a Jewish Christian couple who had most recently come from Rome. They were expelled along with all Jews in AD 49 by decree of the emperor Claudius. Roman historians describe civil disturbances in the capital city over a certain "Chrestus," probably a Latin spelling of Christ. The uprisings were probably caused by debates among the Jews about whether Jesus was the Christ. Paul makes an immediate connection with the couple because they share the same occupation: "by trade they were tentmakers" (verse 3). The profession of tentmaker includes a variety of skills working with canvas and leather. Paul finds both lodging and work with them. Most probably their shop becomes a place of teaching and discussion during the week, while Paul preaches in the synagogue on the Sabbath. Priscilla and Aquila will play an important role in Paul's life, and he refers to them throughout Paul's letters.

Paul's work meets with some early success: "Many of the Corinthians who heard Paul became believers and were baptized" (verse 8). These include Titius Justus, a worshiper of God who lives next door to the synagogue, and Crispus, the synagogue ruler who comes to the faith with his household. But Paul's success arouses the hostility of many of the Jews in the synagogue, and Paul is forced to withdraw and focus his attention on the Gentiles. He shakes the dust from his clothes, a symbolic action telling the Jews that he is no longer responsible for their fate. In spite of the risks, Paul is assured by a vision from the Lord Jesus, urging him not to fear but to keep on speaking, and promising him that he will be protected from harm.

A few months later, the Jewish population launched an attack and brought Paul before the tribunal for judgment. They accuse him of "persuading people to worship God in ways that are contrary to the law" (verse 13). Just as Paul is about to speak in his defense, Gallio cuts him short and dismisses the charges. He judges that the Jews should settle the matter themselves, since the debate is over issues concerning the Hebrew Scriptures. The Christian faith is not a threat to the civil administration of the empire. The response of the Roman governor is not unlike the way that Pilate handled Jesus. This incident may be the beginning of Paul's realization that the Roman government could be his protection.

Reflection and discussion

• Paul's stay in Athens lasted only a few weeks, while his stay in Corinth was eighteen months in length. What might be some of the reasons why Luke's account of Paul's stay in each city is about the same length?

• Why would Luke want to demonstrate that Christianity is not a threat to the government of the Roman Empire?

• Sosthenes, the official of the synagogue, is mentioned only here in Acts (verse 17), but his name is found again at the beginning of Paul's first letter to the Corinthians (1:1). What might have happened to Sosthenes after his beating?

Prayer

Lord Jesus, you protected Paul and urged him to continue teaching the word of God. Teach me not to be afraid to be a witness for you, and show me how to demonstrate the good news of your salvation with my life.

When Priscilla and Aquila heard him, they took him aside and explained the Way of God to him more accurately. Acts 18:26

Apollos Learns to Proclaim the Way

ACTS 18:18-28 *¹⁸After staying there for a considerable time, Paul said farewell to the believers and sailed for Syria, accompanied by Priscilla and Aquila. At Cenchreae he had his hair cut, for he was under a vow. ¹⁹When they reached Ephesus, he left them there, but first he himself went into the synagogue and had a discussion with the Jews. ²⁰When they asked him to stay longer, he declined; ²¹but on taking leave of them, he said, "I will return to you, if God wills." Then he set sail from Ephesus.*

²²When he had landed at Caesarea, he went up to Jerusalem and greeted the church, and then went down to Antioch. ²³After spending some time there he departed and went from place to place through the region of Galatia and Phrygia, strengthening all the disciples.

²⁴Now there came to Ephesus a Jew named Apollos, a native of Alexandria. He was an eloquent man, well-versed in the scriptures. ²⁵He had been instructed in the Way of the Lord; and he spoke with burning enthusiasm and taught accurately the things concerning Jesus, though he knew only the baptism of John. ²⁶He began to speak boldly in the synagogue; but when Priscilla and Aquila heard

him, they took him aside and explained the Way of God to him more accurately.
*²⁷And when he wished to cross over to Achaia, the believers encouraged him and
wrote to the disciples to welcome him. On his arrival he greatly helped those who
through grace had become believers, ²⁸for he powerfully refuted the Jews in public, showing by the scriptures that the Messiah is Jesus.*

This summary account narrates the end of Paul's second missionary
journey with almost breathless haste. At the port city of Cenchreae,
Paul has his hair cut as part of a vow to God for keeping him safe,
demonstrating that Paul still practices the religious customs of Judaism.
Boarding a ship, he travels with Priscilla and Aquila to Ephesus, a great com-
mercial city in Asia Minor.

He leaves his companions there with the city's large Jewish population, and
when the members of the synagogue ask him to stay longer, he promises to
return to them, if God wills it. In fact, Ephesus will be the center of Paul's next
mission. Sailing again, Paul disembarks at Caesarea; then he goes up to
Jerusalem to visit with the church there. And finally Paul returns to Antioch,
where his journey had begun.

Before Paul returns to Ephesus on his next journey, Luke sets the stage by
introducing his readers to Apollos (verse 24). He is a well-educated and eloquent Jew from Alexandria. Well versed in the Jewish Scriptures, he understands how God's saving plan leads to the promises about the Messiah. Having
been "instructed in the Way of the Lord," Apollos seems to already be a
believer when he arrives in Ephesus, and he speaks about Jesus with boldness
and enthusiasm.

Yet, despite the ability of Apollos to teach, his understanding of the
Christian faith is lacking in some ways. Knowing only the baptism of John,
Apollos does not understand the gift of the Holy Spirit given to the church or
his own ability to receive God's Spirit in Christian baptism. His teaching is not
inaccurate, but it is incomplete.

When Priscilla and Aquila hear Apollos teaching in the synagogue, they
take him aside and begin to carefully explain to him the full benefits of salvation offered by God (verse 26). "The Way of God" designates the teachings
that run through the early speeches of Acts, namely, that God has fulfilled the
promises foretold by the prophets in the life, death, resurrection, and ascen-

sion of Jesus and in the gift of the Holy Spirit. Apollos then uses his new understanding of the gospel and his own knowledge of the ancient Scriptures to proclaim and teach the new faith.

When Apollos later desires to minister in Greece, the believers in Ephesus encourage him and write letters of introduction and commendation for him. Apollos proves to be a great help for those who have become believers there, and he uses his rich knowledge of Scripture to demonstrate persuasively that the Messiah is Jesus. His learning and eloquence make him an effective minister of the gospel, and Paul reveals in his first letter to the Corinthians that he considered Apollos a friend and a valued colleague (1 Cor 3:6).

Reflection and discussion

• One task of the church is teaching and equipping believers to evangelize. How does the partnership of Priscilla and Aquila carry out this important task for Apollos? What can married couples learn from them?

• Apollos used his knowledge of Scripture to proclaim the gospel to others. How can a deeper understanding of the Bible help me to do the church's work of evangelization?

Prayer

Lord God, your written word offers me inspiring models of service. Give me some of the zeal and devotion of Paul, Priscilla, Aquila, and Apollos so that I can use wisely the gifts you have given to me.

This continued for two years, so that all the residents of Asia, both Jews and Greeks, heard the word of the Lord. Acts 19:10

Paul's Mission in Ephesus

ACTS 19:1-20 *¹While Apollos was in Corinth, Paul passed through the interior regions and came to Ephesus, where he found some disciples. ²He said to them, "Did you receive the Holy Spirit when you became believers?" They replied, "No, we have not even heard that there is a Holy Spirit." ³Then he said, "Into what then were you baptized?" They answered, "Into John's baptism." ⁴Paul said, "John baptized with the baptism of repentance, telling the people to believe in the one who was to come after him, that is, in Jesus." ⁵On hearing this, they were baptized in the name of the Lord Jesus. ⁶When Paul had laid his hands on them, the Holy Spirit came upon them, and they spoke in tongues and prophesied—⁷altogether there were about twelve of them.*

⁸He entered the synagogue and for three months spoke out boldly, and argued persuasively about the kingdom of God. ⁹When some stubbornly refused to believe and spoke evil of the Way before the congregation, he left them, taking the disciples with him, and argued daily in the lecture hall of Tyrannus. ¹⁰This continued for two years, so that all the residents of Asia, both Jews and Greeks, heard the word of the Lord.

[11]God did extraordinary miracles through Paul, [12]so that when the handkerchiefs or aprons that had touched his skin were brought to the sick, their diseases left them, and the evil spirits came out of them. [13]Then some itinerant Jewish exorcists tried to use the name of the Lord Jesus over those who had evil spirits, saying, "I adjure you by the Jesus whom Paul proclaims." [14]Seven sons of a Jewish high priest named Sceva were doing this. [15]But the evil spirit said to them in reply, "Jesus I know, and Paul I know; but who are you?" [16]Then the man with the evil spirit leaped on them, mastered them all, and so overpowered them that they fled out of the house naked and wounded. [17]When this became known to all residents of Ephesus, both Jews and Greeks, everyone was awestruck; and the name of the Lord Jesus was praised. [18]Also many of those who became believers confessed and disclosed their practices. [19]A number of those who practiced magic collected their books and burned them publicly; when the value of these books was calculated, it was found to come to fifty thousand silver coins. [20]So the word of the Lord grew mightily and prevailed.

Ephesus is another of those cities in which Paul settles for an extended time—probably about three years in all (20:31). The city was magnificent, the capital of the Roman province of Asia. The excavated ruins of Ephesus lie in today's western Turkey. Much of what we learn about the city from Luke is confirmed by other ancient literature and archaeological evidence. The city was renowned for its massive temple to the goddess Artemis. The temple drew great numbers of pilgrims and was an important part of the city's abundant commerce. Ephesus was also a center for the imperial cult, earning it the title of "temple keeper."

When Paul comes to Ephesus, he first encounters a group of believers who, like Apollos, have only received the baptism of John. They have not been taught about the work of the Holy Spirit. They know about Jesus, but they need a more complete understanding of the fullness of salvation that he offers through the Spirit.

Paul explains that John's baptism expressed repentance, but it was only a preparation for the Messiah who would baptize with the Holy Spirit. With their new understanding, they are all baptized "in the name of the Lord Jesus," and Paul lays his hands on them, invoking the Holy Spirit (verses 5-6). Paul's sacramental action in Ephesus bestows the Spirit, just as the apostles Peter and John had invoked the Spirit upon the new believers in Samaria.

Paul follows his usual pattern of preaching first in the synagogue. His primary theme is "the kingdom of God," another way of speaking about the reign God establishes through Jesus the Messiah (verse 8). The focus on God's kingdom may be particularly confrontational in Ephesus, where the Roman emperor is worshipped as the savior and ruler of a worldwide kingdom. While Paul speaks out boldly, some refuse to believe and they publicly malign the new Way.

After three months, Paul moves his evangelizing ministry to a public lecture hall owned by Tyrannus. Here, with a wider audience, he is able to proclaim "the word of the Lord" to all the Jewish and Greek residents of the region (verse 10). As people come to Ephesus for trade, Roman festivals, and worship of the goddess, they are drawn into the sphere of Paul's preaching, and then as they return home to the smaller cities of the province, the new faith radiates out to all of Asia Minor.

The healing miracles that God works through Paul are distinguished from the magic that was so rampant in Ephesus. Whereas magic seeks to manipulate the gods, expecting specific results based on the use of spells, powerful names, and coercion, miracle is God's sovereign act performed through a mediator.

The failure of the seven sons of Sceva to use the name of the Lord Jesus to expel evil spirits demonstrates the distinction between miracle and magic. They do not believe in the gospel Paul preaches, yet they try to tap into his power. Their attempts to manipulate the name of Jesus fail to expel the evil spirits. In fact, the spirits indicate their respect for Jesus and Paul, but they leap on the charlatans and overwhelm them, driving them naked and wounded from the house.

Following this incident, many praise the name of Jesus and become believers. Those who have been practicing magic confess their deeds and divulge their secret spells. As a sign of the changed direction of their lives, they renounce their superstitions and voluntarily burn the books containing their magical formulas. The high monetary value of the books contrasts with the priceless value of the new faith they have embraced. The result is that "the word of the Lord" spread widely and continued to grow in power.

Reflection and discussion

• What are the main differences between the power to heal and exorcise demons given by the Holy Spirit and the magical powers performed by many in Ephesus?

• Why did the sons of Sceva fail when they tried to use the name of Jesus for their own ends? How do people today try to use Jesus for their own purposes?

• What would I need to burn or destroy in order to faithfully practice my Christian faith? What would it cost me to do so?

Prayer

Lord Jesus, you heal and save all who call upon your name. Help me to set aside all counterfeit powers that seek my allegiance and to place my trust in you. May I seek first the kingdom of God above all else.

"You also see and hear that not only in Ephesus but in almost the whole of Asia this Paul has persuaded and drawn away a considerable number of people by saying that gods made with hands are not gods." Acts 19:26

The Riot of the Silversmiths

ACTS 19:21-41 *²¹Now after these things had been accomplished, Paul resolved in the Spirit to go through Macedonia and Achaia, and then to go on to Jerusalem. He said, "After I have gone there, I must also see Rome." ²²So he sent two of his helpers, Timothy and Erastus, to Macedonia, while he himself stayed for some time longer in Asia.*

²³About that time no little disturbance broke out concerning the Way. ²⁴A man named Demetrius, a silversmith who made silver shrines of Artemis, brought no little business to the artisans. ²⁵These he gathered together, with the workers of the same trade, and said, "Men, you know that we get our wealth from this business. ²⁶You also see and hear that not only in Ephesus but in almost the whole of Asia this Paul has persuaded and drawn away a considerable number of people by saying that gods made with hands are not gods. ²⁷And there is danger not only that this trade of ours may come into disrepute but also that the temple of the great goddess Artemis will be scorned, and she will be deprived of her majesty that brought all Asia and the world to worship her."

²⁸When they heard this, they were enraged and shouted, "Great is Artemis of the Ephesians!" ²⁹The city was filled with the confusion; and people rushed together to the theater, dragging with them Gaius and Aristarchus, Macedonians who were Paul's travel companions. [30] Paul wished to go into the crowd, but the disciples would not let him; [31] even some officials of the province of Asia, who were friendly to him, sent him a message urging him not to venture into the theater. [32] Meanwhile, some were shouting one thing, some another; for the assembly was in confusion, and most of them did not know why they had come together. [33] Some of the crowd gave instructions to Alexander, whom the Jews had pushed forward. And Alexander motioned for silence and tried to make a defense before the people. [34] But when they recognized that he was a Jew, for about two hours all of them shouted in unison, "Great is Artemis of the Ephesians!" [35] But when the town clerk had quieted the crowd, he said, "Citizens of Ephesus, who is there that does not know that the city of the Ephesians is the temple keeper of the great Artemis and of the statue that fell from heaven? [36] Since these things cannot be denied, you ought to be quiet and do nothing rash. [37] You have brought these men here who are neither temple robbers nor blasphemers of our goddess. [38] If therefore Demetrius and the artisans with him have a complaint against anyone, the courts are open, and there are proconsuls; let them bring charges there against one another. [39] If there is anything further you want to know, it must be settled in the regular assembly. [40] For we are in danger of being charged with rioting today, since there is no cause that we can give to justify this commotion." [41] When he had said this, he dismissed the assembly.

Artemis, the multi-breasted, fertile mother goddess, was worshiped at shrines in many cities, but the principal site for her honor was at Ephesus. Her temple was four times the size of the Parthenon at Athens and designated as one of the seven wonders of the ancient world. Festivals for the goddess attracted thousands of visitors, especially the week-long spring festival, known as Artemision. Archaeologists have uncovered statues of the goddess, coins with representations of her temple, and terracotta reproductions of the temple. The array of commerce built around her was a major driver of the city's thriving economy.

In this dramatic scene, a silversmith named Demetrius, who crafts silver shrines of Artemis, calls together the artisans of the city who make their living from crafts related to the cult of Artemis. He knows that Paul's message is a threat to their livelihood. If Paul continues to persuade people throughout the region that "gods made with hands are not gods," then not only is their trade at risk but the temple of Artemis is in danger of being scorned (verses 26-27). Demetrius knows how to stir up a crowd, and he appeals to the religious devotion of the Ephesians: the great goddess "will be deprived of her majesty that brought all Asia and the world to worship her." His rhetoric raises the fury of the crowd and they all chant, "Great is Artemis of the Ephesians!" (verse 28). The enraged crowd spills into the streets, shouting and gathering more people as they move, converging on the huge and acoustically perfect amphitheater of Ephesus.

Although idolatry has become a way of life for the Gentiles of the city, Paul has convinced many of them to leave such practice behind. And because Paul's preaching has extended far beyond Ephesus as well, the message of the gospel for all nations seems to be in direct conflict with the real-world financial and political concerns of the empire. The scene shows how greed, acquisitiveness, and self-protection combine with the civic pride of the city's inhabitants to produce violent emotions, noise and confusion, throngs in the streets, and mob justice.

Paul desires to go into the theater, but his disciples and supporters in the city urge him not to venture into the gathering. They are concerned for Paul's safety, and they know that the situation may become even more chaotic if Paul dives in. Confusion abounds, with some shouting one thing, some another. When a Jew named Alexander comes forward to make a defense, he is shouted down by the crowd. Perhaps he wants to make a distinction between the Jews of the synagogue and the Christians so that the violence does not spill over into blaming all Jews.

Only the town clerk, the highest civic official of the city, is able to quiet the crowd and pacify the situation. He addresses the city as one who shares its interests. As "the temple keeper of the great Artemis," the city is known far and wide. He notes that the Christians have committed no act of violence against the goddess and have not blasphemed her. Arguing that civil law and order must be kept, he suggests that if Artemis is really a goddess, then there is no reason to be concerned about her loss of majesty or demise. His level-headed words are reminiscent of the statements of Gamaliel about the new believers in Jerusalem (5:33-39).

The clerk urges the people to come to the courts or to the regularly-held legal assemblies of the citizenry if they have a complaint. He fears that the lawless mob will be arrested by the Romans for rioting without a legal cause. In that case, the Roman authorities could limit the status of Ephesus as a free city. The crowd heeds his words and they leave without rioting.

In describing this event, Luke contrasts the chaos created by the followers of the pagan gods and goddesses with the persuasive teaching and peaceful order produced by Paul and the disciples. The riotous scene in the theater stands out against the Christian assembly depicted throughout Acts as united in mind and heart, witnessing their faith, joined at table, and sharing possessions. Paul taught always in the form of persuasive discussion, never imposing the faith on anyone. He makes his case not through a quick and emotional appeal, but by helping people gain an appreciation for the gospel. He stays with them, engaging in their context, continuing to teach, and he sets up ministers in the new communities before he departs from them. Luke demonstrates through these events that Paul's style of evangelization is not a threat to the empire and has no reason to be opposed.

Reflection and discussion

• Why does Demetrius feel so threatened by the teachings of Paul? In what ways does the gospel of Jesus challenge the financial and political concerns of our society today?

• In Ephesus the worship of Artemis became the source of the city's economic gain. What are some of the positive and negative implications of this tendency in religion today?

• In what ways are the concerns of Demetrius and those of the town clerk different? How is the wisdom of the town clerk similar to that of Gamaliel (5:33-39)?

• How does the riotous scene in the theater demonstrate some of the fanatical tendencies in religion?

• Some of today's cultural idols are money, success, power, and possessions. What is one way I can transfer my loyalty from a cultural idol to the Lord of my life?

Prayer

Lord Jesus, you have come into our world and have shown us how to exist in the midst of the idols that surround us. Do not let greed or selfish desires diminish my devotion to you, but teach me to submit all things in this passing world to you.

SUGGESTIONS FOR FACILITATORS, GROUP SESSION 3

1. Welcome group members and ask if there are any announcements anyone would like to make.

2. You may want to pray this prayer as a group:

Father of our Lord Jesus Christ, your word offers us inspiring models of evangelization in the figures of Paul, Silas, Timothy, Priscilla, Aquila, and Apollos. Although they were charged with turning the world upside down, their devotion to the gospel and faithful teaching demonstrates their desire that the world be saved in Christ. As we continue to study the Scriptures, show us how to evangelize and teach others the salvation made known through your Holy Spirit. Help us to set aside all idols that seek our allegiance and to place our loyal trust in Jesus Christ your Son.

3. Ask one or more of the following questions:
   - Which image from lessons 7–12 stands out most memorably to you?
   - What is the most important thing you learned through your study this week?

4. Discuss lessons 7 through 12. Choose one or more of the questions for reflection and discussion from each lesson to discuss as a group. You may want to ask group members which question was most challenging or helpful to them as you review each lesson.

5. Remember that there are no definitive answers for these discussion questions. The insights of group members will add to the understanding of all. None of these questions require an expert.

6. After talking about each lesson, instruct group members to complete lessons 13 through 18 on their own during the six days before the next group meeting. They should write out their own answers to the questions as preparation for next week's group discussion.

7. Ask the group if anyone is having any particular problems with the Bible study during the week. You may want to share advice and encouragement within the group.

8. Conclude by praying aloud together the prayer at the end of one of the lessons discussed. You may add to the prayer based on the sharing that has occurred in the group.

On the first day of the week, when we met to break bread,
Paul was holding a discussion with them; since he intended
to leave the next day, he continued speaking until midnight. Acts 20:7

Paul Teaches
the Church in Troas

ACTS 20:1-16 *¹After the uproar had ceased, Paul sent for the disciples; and after encouraging them and saying farewell, he left for Macedonia. ²When he had gone through those regions and had given the believers much encouragement, he came to Greece, ³where he stayed for three months. He was about to set sail for Syria when a plot was made against him by the Jews, and so he decided to return through Macedonia. ⁴He was accompanied by Sopater son of Pyrrhus from Beroea, by Aristarchus and Secundus from Thessalonica, by Gaius from Derbe, and by Timothy, as well as by Tychicus and Trophimus from Asia. ⁵They went ahead and were waiting for us in Troas; ⁶but we sailed from Philippi after the days of Unleavened Bread, and in five days we joined them in Troas, where we stayed for seven days.*

⁷On the first day of the week, when we met to break bread, Paul was holding a discussion with them; since he intended to leave the next day, he continued speaking until midnight. ⁸There were many lamps in the room upstairs where we were meeting. ⁹A young man named Eutychus, who was sitting in the window, began to sink off into a deep sleep while Paul talked still longer. Overcome by sleep, he fell to the ground three floors below and was picked up dead. ¹⁰But Paul went down, and bending over him took him in his arms, and said, "Do not be alarmed, for his life is in him." ¹¹Then Paul went upstairs, and after he had broken bread and eaten, he continued to converse with them until dawn; then he left. ¹²Meanwhile they had taken the boy away alive and were not a little comforted.

¹³We went ahead to the ship and set sail for Assos, intending to take Paul on board there; for he had made this arrangement, intending to go by land himself. ¹⁴When he met us in Assos, we took him on board and went to Mitylene. ¹⁵We sailed from there, and on the following day we arrived opposite Chios. The next day we touched at Samos, and the day after that we came to Miletus. ¹⁶For Paul had decided to sail past Ephesus, so that he might not have to spend time in Asia; he was eager to be in Jerusalem, if possible, on the day of Pentecost.

After taking leave of the tense situation in Ephesus, Paul travels through various locations to strengthen and encourage the churches. After passing through Macedonia, he stays for three months during the winter in Greece. Luke lists seven coworkers who are traveling with Paul, mostly with Greek names. These represent some of his most faithful followers from his wide-ranging mission. Here the "we" passages begin again, possibly indicating that Luke too was with Paul. They celebrate the Jewish feast of Unleavened Bread in Philippi, then they sail for five days to Troas. By this time, Paul is on his own journey of divine destiny to Jerusalem and then to Rome, a decision he had made in Ephesus: "Paul resolved in the Spirit to go through Macedonia and Achaia, and then to go to Jerusalem." Then Paul said, "After I have gone there, I must see Rome" (19:21). Paul's determination to go toward his destiny functions in Acts in the same way that Jesus' announcement to journey toward Jerusalem functions in Luke's gospel (Luke 9:51).

Although Paul continues to gather in synagogues on the Sabbath, here is clear evidence that Sunday has become the Christian day of worship. "The first day of the week" was the day of the Lord's resurrection, when the community would assemble to celebrate Eucharist (verse 7). At this particular service, Paul's preaching and teaching goes long into the night because he is leaving them the next morning. Luke paints the scene with vivid details and gentle humor. A youth named Eutychus, whose name means "good fortune" or "lucky," is sitting in the window of the third-floor room in which the church is meeting. Because of the late hour, the many oil lamps that depleted the room's oxygen, and Paul's incessant sermon, Eutychus goes to sleep and falls to the ground (verse 9).

Paul descends to the boy, embraces him, and pronounces him alive. The boy's resuscitation is set in the context of the Lord's day, when the community remembers the dying and rising of Jesus and his invitation to new life. The power of Christ's resurrection is at work in Paul as he revives Eutychus. Luke makes the connection with references to a "room upstairs," the first day of the week, and the breaking of the bread—all elements of the disciples' experiences of Christ's resurrection at the end of Luke's gospel.

As Paul continues his long and final journey to Jerusalem, he travels first from Troas to Assos by land, while his coworkers sail by ship. Then boarding the ship, they all travel southward with short trips from port to port, typical of ancient sea trips. They must proceed cautiously because the winds and rocky coast are difficult to navigate. Because Paul desires to be in Jerusalem for the feast of Pentecost, he does not stop to visit Ephesus. Yet, arriving in Miletus, a coastal city near Ephesus, Paul sends a message to the elders of the church in Ephesus to meet him there.

Reflection and discussion

• What have I learned about Paul's character in reading the narratives of his travels?

• When do I feel like Eutychus? How can I be more spiritually awake?

• Although the Torah of Israel states that the day of rest is the last day of the week, Christians worshiped God on the "first day of the week." What are some reasons why the Lord's Day is the week's first day?

• Why did Paul continue speaking until midnight? When was the last time I discussed something until midnight?

• What are the similarities between Paul's determination to travel toward his destiny and Jesus' resolve to journey to Jerusalem (Luke 9:51)? Why does Luke show this clear parallel?

Prayer

Lord Jesus, you called Paul to the ministry of proclaiming your good news to the world. Give me a taste of his passionate zeal for the gospel, and give me the courage to strive toward my life's goal.

"Keep watch over yourselves and over all the flock, of which the Holy Spirit has made you overseers, to shepherd the church of God that he obtained with the blood of his own Son." Acts 20:28

Paul's Farewell to the Ephesian Elders

ACTS 20:17-38 *[17]From Miletus he sent a message to Ephesus, asking the elders of the church to meet him. [18]When they came to him, he said to them:*

"You yourselves know how I lived among you the entire time from the first day that I set foot in Asia, [19]serving the Lord with all humility and with tears, enduring the trials that came to me through the plots of the Jews. [20]I did not shrink from doing anything helpful, proclaiming the message to you and teaching you publicly and from house to house, [21]as I testified to both Jews and Greeks about repentance toward God and faith toward our Lord Jesus. [22]And now, as a captive to the Spirit, I am on my way to Jerusalem, not knowing what will happen to me there,[23]except that the Holy Spirit testifies to me in every city that imprisonment and persecutions are waiting for me. [24]But I do not count my life of any value to myself, if only I may finish my course and the ministry that I received from the Lord Jesus, to testify to the good news of God's grace.

[25]"And now I know that none of you, among whom I have gone about proclaiming the kingdom, will ever see my face again. [26]Therefore I declare to you this day that I am not responsible for the blood of any of you, [27]for I did not shrink from declaring to you the whole purpose of God. [28]Keep watch over your-

selves and over all the flock, of which the Holy Spirit has made you overseers, to shepherd the church of God that he obtained with the blood of his own Son. ²⁹I know that after I have gone, savage wolves will come in among you, not sparing the flock. ³⁰Some even from your own group will come distorting the truth in order to entice the disciples to follow them. ³¹Therefore be alert, remembering that for three years I did not cease night or day to warn everyone with tears. ³²And now I commend you to God and to the message of his grace, a message that is able to build you up and to give you the inheritance among all who are sanctified. ³³I coveted no one's silver or gold or clothing. ³⁴You know for yourselves that I worked with my own hands to support myself and my companions. ³⁵In all this I have given you an example that by such work we must support the weak, remembering the words of the Lord Jesus, for he himself said, 'It is more blessed to give than to receive.'"

³⁶When he had finished speaking, he knelt down with them all and prayed. ³⁷There was much weeping among them all; they embraced Paul and kissed him, ³⁸grieving especially because of what he had said, that they would not see him again. Then they brought him to the ship.

Pausing during his long and final journey to Jerusalem, Paul meets with the elders of the church in Ephesus before he departs from them for the last time. After summoning them to Miletus near the coast, he offers them a heartfelt farewell address, offering his listeners a more intimate portrait of himself than his frantic pace of travels has until now allowed. The parallels are numerous between Paul's address to the elders and the farewell discourse of Jesus with his disciples (Luke 22:14-38). Like Jesus, the "one who serves," Paul presents the pattern of his own life as the model for their imitation. He warns them about the difficulties that lie ahead and prepares them for the suffering to come.

Like Jesus, Paul predicts his own passion while on his way to Jerusalem. He walks the path to suffering "as a captive to the Spirit" (verse 22). The former persecutor, who wanted to bring bound captives to Jerusalem, is now a captive of God's Spirit, divinely compelled to move toward that city. There imprisonment and persecution await him (verse 23). Just as dark clouds gathered during the final chapters of Jesus' journey, Paul's life too will come to a somber end with trial and affliction. He knows he has been called to suffer on behalf of the gospel he preaches (9:16). Yet, Paul's only desire is to finish the course, to complete the task given to him by the risen Lord (verse 24). He summarizes his proclamation to the nations as "the good news of God's grace." He is willing to forego even life itself for the sake of that saving gospel.

Paul expresses his deep love for the people of the church in Ephesus and shows that their pastoral care is the center of his concerns. His own pastoral role has now ended, and the Ephesian elders are to carry on as shepherds of the flock. Addressing words of counsel to his successors in the church's leadership, he urges the church's elders to be models to those under their care, and he offers himself as an example for their imitation. The exemplary lives of Christ's ministers testify to the genuineness of the gospel.

Paul stresses both the sacredness and the precariousness of the elders' pastoral duty. They have been given their task as "overseers" of the flock by the Holy Spirit. The dangers to the flock are expressed with the image of the "savage wolves," menacing the church from the outside and from within (verses 29-30). False teachers and unworthy leaders will seduce the church and draw disciples to themselves rather than to Christ.

Paul connects the example of his own ministry and his exhortation to the elders with the life of Jesus, the ultimate model for imitation. He offers a saying of Jesus not recorded in any of the four gospels: "It is more blessed to give than to receive" (verse 35). Church leaders have a responsibility to give of themselves and to "support the weak" after the model of Jesus the Shepherd.

This farewell speech foreshadows the end of Paul's missionary activity and hints at his suffering and future martyrdom for Christ. The final leave-taking involves praying, weeping, embracing, kissing, and grieving (verses 36-38). This emotional scene expresses the deep affection that must bind together every Christian community and the sense of loving responsibility passed from the generation of the apostles to the leaders of the church in every age.

Reflection and discussion

• What do I want to accomplish at any cost? How do my life's goals compare to the desire of Paul as expressed in verse 24?

• The church always needs its saints as models of holy living and dying. What characteristics of Paul's ministry does he offer as an example to the elders of Ephesus?

• Paul urges the elders at Ephesus to "keep watch" (verse 28) and "be alert" (verse 31). What does Paul mean by these two imperatives for the church and its leaders?

• Paul's address offers us words of Jesus that are not recorded in any gospel: "It is more blessed to give than to receive." How did Jesus demonstrate this truth in his own life? How have I discovered the meaning of his words?

Prayer

Good Shepherd, watch over your church and guide those who lead it. Help me to follow the example of Paul, imitate his pastoral concern for the weak, give myself in service of others, and care for those in need.

"What are you doing, weeping and breaking my heart?
For I am ready not only to be bound but even to die in Jerusalem
for the name of the Lord Jesus." Acts 21:13

Prophecy of Suffering to Come

ACTS 21:1-16 *¹When we had parted from them and set sail, we came by a straight course to Cos, and the next day to Rhodes, and from there to Patara. ²When we found a ship bound for Phoenicia, we went on board and set sail. ³We came in sight of Cyprus; and leaving it on our left, we sailed to Syria and landed at Tyre, because the ship was to unload its cargo there. ⁴We looked up the disciples and stayed there for seven days. Through the Spirit they told Paul not to go on to Jerusalem. ⁵When our days there were ended, we left and proceeded on our journey; and all of them, with wives and children, escorted us outside the city. There we knelt down on the beach and prayed ⁶and said farewell to one another. Then we went on board the ship, and they returned home.*

⁷When we had finished the voyage from Tyre, we arrived at Ptolemais; and we greeted the believers and stayed with them for one day. ⁸The next day we left and came to Caesarea; and we went into the house of Philip the evangelist, one of the seven, and stayed with him. ⁹He had four unmarried daughters who had the gift of prophecy. ¹⁰While we were staying there for several days, a prophet named Agabus came down from Judea. ¹¹He came to us and took Paul's belt, bound his own feet and hands with it, and said, "Thus says the Holy Spirit, 'This is the way the Jews in Jerusalem will bind the man who owns this belt and will hand him over to the Gentiles.'" [12]When we heard this, we and the people there urged him not to go up to Jerusalem. [13]Then Paul answered, "What are you doing, weeping and breaking my heart? For I am ready not only to be bound but even to die in Jerusalem for the name of the Lord Jesus." [14]Since he would not be persuaded, we remained silent except to say, "The Lord's will be done."

[15]After these days we got ready and started to go up to Jerusalem. [16]Some of the disciples from Caesarea also came along and brought us to the house of Mnason of Cyprus, an early disciple, with whom we were to stay.

These episodes follow Paul's travel from the tearful departure from Miletus to his arrival in Jerusalem. The section reads like a travel journal, possibly Luke's own chronicle, since the pronoun "we" is used. He describes a series of one-day stops, followed by a longer voyage to Phoenicia on the open sea. When they reach Tyre, the ship unloads its cargo, and Paul remains for a week. He and his companions spend their days visiting disciples, who express their concern about Paul's well-being and warn him not to go on to Jerusalem. When they depart from Tyre, the whole families of the believers escort them from the city. When they all reach the beach, they kneel down and pray, then bid farewell to one another.

After a few days, Paul and his companions arrive in Caesarea, the major port city founded by Herod the Great. Paul lodges there at the house of Philip and his four unmarried daughters who are prophets. While there, another prophet, Agabus, arrives from Judea. Earlier in Jerusalem, Agabus had accurately predicted a worldwide famine (11:28). Now he offers a warning to Paul in the form of a vivid prophecy. Like the ancient prophets Jeremiah and Ezekiel, Agabus expresses his prophecy through symbolic gestures, using Paul's belt to enact the oracle he speaks. Wrapping the belt around his own hands and feet, Agabus says through the Holy Spirit, "This is the way the Jews in Jerusalem will bind the man who owns this belt and will hand him over to the Gentiles." The prophecy echoes Jesus' own predictions of his passion in the gospels.

As in the farewell scene at Miletus, the emotional intensity of the departure is high. Paul has generated love and loyalty among his followers. Yet, despite the weeping and urging of his companions and the people of Caesarea that he not go to Jerusalem, Paul is determined to follow the Lord's will and continue his journey to the holy city (verses 12-13). Paul's anguish does not deter him from expressing his willingness to suffer and even to die "for the name of the Lord Jesus." Once his companions understand that Paul is being driven by the Spirit to face what is ahead, they embrace the path and support him, seeking only God's will.

Paul and his companions continue the final leg of their travel toward Jerusalem. He has repeatedly heard from the Spirit what faces him there, and he is ready for what is to come. He will testify to Jesus, no matter the results. Arriving in Jerusalem, Paul's final missionary journey ends.

Reflection and discussion

• Why did Agabus choose to act out his prophecy? What are some of the echoes from the passion of Jesus in this passage about Paul?

• Did Paul make the right decision to go to Jerusalem, even though many urged him not to go? How do I discern God's will when I make critical decisions?

Prayer

Lord Jesus, Paul followed you in living out God's will through his mission, and he sought God's will for each new move. Teach me to discern God's will for my own life, and give me the courage to follow it.

"Fellow Israelites, help! This is the man who is teaching everyone
everywhere against our people, our law, and this place;
more than that, he has actually brought Greeks into the temple
and has defiled this holy place." Acts 21:28

Paul's Return to Jerusalem and Arrest

ACTS 21:17-36 *17When we arrived in Jerusalem, the brothers welcomed us warmly. 18The next day Paul went with us to visit James; and all the elders were present. 19After greeting them, he related one by one the things that God had done among the Gentiles through his ministry. 20When they heard it, they praised God. Then they said to him, "You see, brother, how many thousands of believers there are among the Jews, and they are all zealous for the law. 21They have been told about you that you teach all the Jews living among the Gentiles to forsake Moses, and that you tell them not to circumcise their children or observe the customs. 22What then is to be done? They will certainly hear that you have come. 23So do what we tell you. We have four men who are under a vow. 24Join these men, go through the rite of purification with them, and pay for the shaving of their heads. Thus all will know that there is nothing in what they have been told about you, but that you yourself observe and guard the law. 25But as for the Gentiles who have become believers, we have sent a letter with our judgment that they should abstain from what has been sacrificed to idols and from blood and from what is strangled and from fornication." 26Then Paul took the men, and the next day, having purified himself, he entered the temple with them, making public the completion of the days of purification when the sacri-fice would be made for each of them.*

²⁷When the seven days were almost completed, the Jews from Asia, who had seen him in the temple, stirred up the whole crowd. They seized him, ²⁸shouting, "Fellow Israelites, help! This is the man who is teaching everyone everywhere against our people, our law, and this place; more than that, he has actually brought Greeks into the temple and has defiled this holy place." ²⁹For they had previously seen Trophimus the Ephesian with him in the city, and they supposed that Paul had brought him into the temple. ³⁰Then all the city was aroused, and the people rushed together. They seized Paul and dragged him out of the temple, and immediately the doors were shut. ³¹While they were trying to kill him, word came to the tribune of the cohort that all Jerusalem was in an uproar. ³²Immediately he took soldiers and centurions and ran down to them. When they saw the tribune and the soldiers, they stopped beating Paul. ³³Then the tribune came, arrested him, and ordered him to be bound with two chains; he inquired who he was and what he had done. ³⁴Some in the crowd shouted one thing, some another; and as he could not learn the facts because of the uproar, he ordered him to be brought into the barracks. ³⁵When Paul came to the steps, the violence of the mob was so great that he had to be carried by the soldiers. ³⁶The crowd that followed kept shouting, "Away with him!"

A s Luke narrates Paul arrival in Jerusalem, he emphasizes the essential continuity between the church in Jerusalem and the mission of Paul to the nations. Paul and his companions are greeted warmly in the city when they arrive, and the next day they meet with James, the overseer of the church in Jerusalem, and the elders of the church there. Paul recounts for them the details of his work among the Gentiles and how God has blessed his mission. The leaders in Jerusalem praise God for the response of the Gentiles to the gospel, acknowledging that this is truly God's work. They also update Paul on the mission of the church in Jerusalem to the Jews. Among them are "many thousands of believers." Paul's return from his missionary travels to the mother church in Jerusalem shows the essential unity of the church's mission both to the Jews and to the Gentiles. This unity in Christ demonstrates that while the church must always reach outside of itself, it must always return to its apostolic roots for approval and guidance.

While the leaders of the church encourage Paul's mission, there has arisen much misunderstanding of Paul's work among many of the Jewish believers in the city. Because these Jewish Christians are zealous not only for Jesus the Messiah but also for the law of Moses, they question Paul's fidelity to his Jewish heritage. They have been told that Paul teaches the Jews living among the Gentiles to forsake Moses, telling them not to circumcise their sons or practice the traditions of Israel (verse 21). In fact, what they have been told misstates the truth about Paul. He has indeed brought the gospel to Gentiles without requiring them to follow the law of Moses, but that does not mean that he no longer follows the Torah or counsels others Jews to disregard it.

As a way to counter some of the false rumors about Paul, the leaders of the church urge Paul to demonstrate his loyalty to Judaism by sponsoring four men in the traditional Nazirite ritual (Num 6:1-21). Paul accompanies them in their purification and brings them into the temple to offer the appropriate sacrifices. In this way, Paul demonstrates his continuing respect for the Torah, with hopes of appeasing his opponents. Paul's utmost concern is his commitment to the unity of the church.

However, the false rumors about Paul continue and the hostility against him intensifies. When some Jewish believers from the province of Asia see Paul in the temple, they seize him and stir up a crowd. They shout, "This is the man who is teaching everyone everywhere against our people, our law, and this place" (verse 28). Because they had seen one of Paul's Gentile companions with him in the city, they jump to the conclusion that he had brought the man into the temple with him. Stone markers create a boundary in the central areas of the temple grounds that Gentiles are forbidden to pass. They charge Paul with desecrating the temple by his action. The crowd drags Paul from the temple and begins to beat him, causing an uproar in the city.

As Paul is hauled out of the temple, Luke states, "Immediately the doors were shut" (verse 30). This is the last scene in Acts that shows the temple of Jerusalem. Throughout the story of Jesus and the early years of his church, the temple expressed the continuity between ancient Israel and its Messiah, Jesus. Paul continues to defend this unity of God's saving plan. Yet, the closing of the temple doors now signifies the parting of the ways between Jews who accept Jesus as the Messiah and those who do not.

When the Roman garrison receives word of the disruption, soldiers and centurions are sent from the Antonia Fortress, overlooking the temple grounds. The tribune arrests Paul and binds him in chains, unable to ascertain who he is or what he has done. Throughout the arrest and trial of Paul, we hear echoes of Jesus' passion. Paul is brought into the barracks, while the shout of the crowd—"Away with him!"—repeats the cry of the crowd at Jesus' trial before Pilate (Luke 23:18).

Reflection and discussion

• What does the return of Paul, the missionary to the Gentiles, to the church in Jerusalem indicate about the apostolic and universal qualities of the church?

• How can I better understand the Jewish roots of the church and honor the tradition of Israel in which it stands?

• Do I follow the way of Jesus even when it means hardship and trial? Have I suffered because my intentions have been misunderstood by others?

Prayer

Suffering Lord, help me to persevere in times of suffering and when I am misunderstood. As I seek the way of unity, teach me also the way of your cross. Give me the determination to live and teach the gospel like Paul.

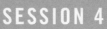
"I am a Jew, born in Tarsus in Cilicia, but brought up in this city
at the feet of Gamaliel, educated strictly according to our ancestral law,
being zealous for God, just as all of you are today." Acts 22:3

Paul's Speech to the People of Jerusalem

ACTS 21:37–22:16 *³⁷Just as Paul was about to be brought into the barracks, he said to the tribune, "May I say something to you?" The tribune replied, "Do you know Greek? ³⁸Then you are not the Egyptian who recently stirred up a revolt and led the four thousand assassins out into the wilderness?" ³⁹Paul replied, "I am a Jew, from Tarsus in Cilicia, a citizen of an important city; I beg you, let me speak to the people." ⁴⁰When he had given him permission, Paul stood on the steps and motioned to the people for silence; and when there was a great hush, he addressed them in the Hebrew language, saying:*

22 ¹"Brothers and fathers, listen to the defense that I now make before you."

²When they heard him addressing them in Hebrew, they became even more quiet. Then he said:

³"I am a Jew, born in Tarsus in Cilicia, but brought up in this city at the feet of Gamaliel, educated strictly according to our ancestral law, being zealous for God, just as all of you are today. ⁴I persecuted this Way up to the point of death by binding both men and women and putting them in prison, ⁵as the high priest and the whole council of elders can testify about me. From them I also received letters to the brothers in Damascus, and I went there in order to bind those who were there and to bring them back to Jerusalem for punishment.

⁶"While I was on my way and approaching Damascus, about noon a great light from heaven suddenly shone about me. ⁷I fell to the ground and heard a voice saying to me, 'Saul, Saul, why are you persecuting me?' ⁸I answered, 'Who are you, Lord?' Then he said to me, 'I am Jesus of Nazareth whom you are persecuting.' ⁹Now those who were with me saw the light but did not hear the voice of the one who was speaking to me. ¹⁰I asked, 'What am I to do, Lord?' The Lord said to me, 'Get up and go to Damascus; there you will be told everything that has been assigned to you to do.' ¹¹Since I could not see because of the brightness of that light, those who were with me took my hand and led me to Damascus.

¹²"A certain Ananias, who was a devout man according to the law and well spoken of by all the Jews living there, ¹³came to me; and standing beside me, he said, 'Brother Saul, regain your sight!' In that very hour I regained my sight and saw him. ¹⁴Then he said, 'The God of our ancestors has chosen you to know his will, to see the Righteous One and to hear his own voice; ¹⁵for you will be his witness to all the world of what you have seen and heard. ¹⁶And now why do you delay? Get up, be baptized, and have your sins washed away, calling on his name.'"

With Paul under arrest and his missionary travels ended, this scene begins Paul's defense and journey to Rome, which will take up the remainder of Acts. His defense is less about defending himself before the Roman authorities and more about defending the Christian faith. In the speeches given by Paul in the final chapters of Acts, he explains how his own calling and ministry to the Gentiles is an integral part of God's saving plan. He defends God's offer of salvation to the Gentiles, which has been narrated in the previous chapters, as the fulfillment of God's original call to Israel. For this reason, Paul's work among the Gentiles has not been his own choice but that of the risen Lord.

As Paul is brought into the barracks of the Antonia Fortress, he requests permission from the tribune to speak to him. The tribune is taken aback when he is addressed in Greek, since he has supposed that Paul is uneducated. He then assumes that Paul must be the last insurrectionist the Romans had to deal with, an Egyptian who tried to attack the city but escaped with some of his followers into the desert. But Paul corrects the tribune, identifying himself as a Jew from Tarsus, one of the great coastal cities in Cilicia. When Paul asks permission to speak to the crowd that is seeking his death, the tribune grants his request.

Motioning with his hands for silence, Paul begins to speak to the people. He is a Jew speaking to his fellow Jews. In an attempt to win their goodwill, he speaks in Hebrew, which probably refers to the Aramaic spoken by most of the Jews of Judea. The crowd grows profoundly silent and listens intently. The speech falls into three parts. First, Paul recounts his earlier life in Judaism (verses 3-5); second, he speaks about the events along the road to Damascus (verses 6-11); and third, he recalls his divine commission to be Christ's witness to all the world (verses 12-16).

Paul begins by proudly stating, "I am a Jew." Though born in Tarsus, he was raised in Jerusalem and was taught the written and oral tradition of Judaism at the feet of the great rabbi Gamaliel. Zealous for God, Paul was educated strictly in the law of Israel. In language, upbringing, and zealotry, Paul was just like his audience. By emphasizing his similarities, Paul implies that he understands what is motivating them. Thus far, Paul presents himself as a devout Jewish Pharisee with unequaled credentials. His religious fervor was so great that he became a persecutor of the Jewish Christians, arresting believers, casting them into prison, and even supporting the death of some.

Next Paul recounts the transforming events that happened to him along the road to Damascus. Though it was noon, when the sun would be most intense, Paul was blinded by a greater light, the glory of God's presence. With Paul prostrate on the ground, a voice asked him why he persecutes him. The voice then identified itself as that of "Jesus of Nazareth whom you are persecuting." The risen Lord then told him to go to Damascus, where he would be told what to do.

The instrument of Paul's divine commission was Ananias, a devout Jewish man in Damascus. Through him, Paul received his sight and then his mission. Ananias told Paul that the God of Israel's past, "the God of our ancestors," had chosen him to be a witness to the will of God in the present. God has chosen him "to know his will, to see the Righteous One and to hear his own voice." Paul is appointed by God to witness to the world what he had seen and heard. So, after being baptized and calling on the Lord's name, Paul's transformed life began.

Reflection and discussion

• Why does Paul recount the events of his life in such detail to the crowd? In what sense is Paul's speech to the crowd less about himself and more about the Way?

• What are some of the ways God prepared Paul from his early life for his divinely given commission?

• If I were called to give testimony for my mission in life, what would I say? What events in my life have led me to a deeper understanding of my life's mission?

Prayer

God of our ancestors, you called Paul to be your instrument for your new work in the world. Keep me rooted in the tradition of the past but always open to the new ways you are guiding my life and your church.

The tribune directed that he was to be brought into the barracks, and ordered him to be examined by flogging, to find out the reason for this outcry against him. Acts 22:24

Paul and the Roman Tribune

ACTS 22:17-29 *¹⁷"After I had returned to Jerusalem and while I was praying in the temple, I fell into a trance ¹⁸and saw Jesus saying to me, 'Hurry and get out of Jerusalem quickly, because they will not accept your testimony about me.' ¹⁹And I said, 'Lord, they themselves know that in every synagogue I imprisoned and beat those who believed in you. ²⁰And while the blood of your witness Stephen was shed, I myself was standing by, approving and keeping the coats of those who killed him.' ²¹Then he said to me, 'Go, for I will send you far away to the Gentiles.'"*

²²Up to this point they listened to him, but then they shouted, "Away with such a fellow from the earth! For he should not be allowed to live." ²³And while they were shouting, throwing off their cloaks, and tossing dust into the air, ²⁴the tribune directed that he was to be brought into the barracks, and ordered him to be examined by flogging, to find out the reason for this outcry against him. ²⁵But when they had tied him up with thongs, Paul said to the centurion who was standing by, "Is it legal for you to flog a Roman citizen who is uncondemned?"

26When the centurion heard that, he went to the tribune and said to him, "What are you about to do? This man is a Roman citizen." 27The tribune came and asked Paul, "Tell me, are you a Roman citizen?" And he said, "Yes." 28The tribune answered, "It cost me a large sum of money to get my citizenship." Paul said, "But I was born a citizen." 29Immediately those who were about to examine him drew back from him; and the tribune also was afraid, for he realized that Paul was a Roman citizen and that he had bound him.

After Paul's speech to the crowds tells of his earlier life in Judaism, recounts the events along the road to Damascus, and recalls his divine commission to be Christ's witness to all the world, Paul adds details not mentioned in the earlier chapters of Acts. Paul's commission that he received through Ananias in Damascus was subsequently confirmed by a vision as he was praying in the temple of Jerusalem. In the vision, Jesus told him to leave Jerusalem quickly because the Jews of the city will not accept his testimony (verse 18).

Paul initially questioned the call to leave Jerusalem, since he thought his persecution of the Christians gave him credibility among the Jews of the city. He thought that if the people were going to listen to anyone it would be to him, for he had gone from one synagogue to another, arresting, jailing, and beating the believers. He had even taken part in the murder of Stephen, approving the act and keeping the coats of those who stoned him. Paul would have preferred to stay in Jerusalem, carrying out God's commission among the Jews of the city. But the Lord told Paul that he had a different calling: "Go, for I will send you far away to the Gentiles" (verse 21).

Paul's testimony about his experience in the temple accomplishes several things in this context. First, Paul's visit to the temple witnesses to his long-standing devotion to the Jewish sanctuary. Second, his prayer in the holy place confirms his belief in the temple as a place for prayer in God's presence. Third, his visionary experience connects him to Peter, to whom God's will was also revealed through visions. And finally, his experience is like that of the prophet Isaiah, who had a vision of the Lord in the temple of Jerusalem and received a commission to be sent. All of these aspects of Paul's commission in the temple validate his oneness with the Jewish tradition and solidify his place in the history of God's salvation.

While the people have listened attentively to Paul up to this point, his mention that the God of Israel has called him to invite the Gentiles into blessings stirs the crowd to anger. They cry that Paul should be taken away and does not deserve to live (verse 22). The reaction is like that against Jesus at his inaugural address in the synagogue of Nazareth (Luke 4:24-30). While Jesus spoke of his solidarity with the prophets, the people listened, but when he spoke of blessings for the Gentiles, the people were filled with rage, drove him out of town, and desired to hurl him off the cliff. For those who listened to both Jesus and Paul, the idea that Gentiles could be acceptable to God on the same basis as the Jews seemed unthinkable.

The Roman commander does not understand the reason for this outcry against Paul, so he decides to bring him into the barracks. He believes that the only way to get at the truth of the matter is to interrogate the prisoner by flogging. Paul is probably on the stone pavement in the central courtyard of the fortress, the same area where Jesus had been brought a generation before. As on that occasion, so now a Roman centurion is in charge of the detail to interrogate Paul. As they stretch him out for scourging, Paul raises the issue of his Roman citizenship. He asks, "Is it legal for you to flog a Roman citizen who is uncondemned?" (verse 25). Paul's question brings an immediate halt to the proceedings, as they question and verify that Paul is indeed a citizen of Rome. Cicero had said, "To bind a Roman citizen is a crime, to flog him an abomination, to slay him is almost an act of murder." They all withdraw from Paul, worried about how they have treated him. The Roman legal system now protects him. He will remain under arrest unjustly, but not physically abused.

Reflection and discussion

• Why would Jesus have chosen to reveal his will for Paul in the temple of Jerusalem?

• The anger of the Jewish people is aroused when Paul mentions his call to the Gentiles. Why would this be a particularly delicate and difficult issue for a people under the oppression of a foreign power?

• In what ways was Paul's status as a Roman citizen an advantage to him in his ministry among the Gentiles? How is my citizenship a benefit for me as an evangelizer?

• Paul thought that he would be an ideal evangelist to the Jews of Jerusalem, but the risen Lord sent him away to the Gentiles. How has God redirected my life in a way I did not expect?

Prayer

Righteous One, you appeared to Saul and called him to preach to the Gentiles. Help me to understand my calling and make me zealous for God and willing to sacrifice for his name.

SUGGESTIONS FOR FACILITATORS, GROUP SESSION 4

1. Welcome group members and ask if anyone has any questions, announcements, or requests.

2. You may want to pray this prayer as a group:

God of ancient Israel, you called Paul of Tarsus to be the instrument for your new work in the world. Following his worldwide ministry to the Gentiles, he journeyed resolutely to meet his fate in Jerusalem. Like your Son Jesus, Paul sought to discern your will and was courageous enough to follow it. Teach me to discern God's will for my own life, and give me the courage to live and teach the gospel like Paul. Keep me rooted in the ancient tradition but always ready for the new ways you are guiding my life and your church. Help me to be faithful to your word despite its challenging demands.

3. Ask one or more of the following questions:
   - What is the most difficult part of this study for you?
   - What insights stand out to you from the lessons this week?

4. Discuss lessons 13 through 18. Choose one or more of the questions for reflection and discussion from each lesson to discuss as a group. You may want to ask group members which question was most challenging or helpful to them as you review each lesson.

5. Keep the discussion moving, but allow time for the questions that provoke the most discussion. Encourage the group members to use "I" language in their responses.

6. After talking over each lesson, instruct group members to complete lessons 19 through 24 on their own during the six days before the next group meeting. They should write out their own answers to the questions as preparation for next week's session.

7. Ask the group what encouragement they need for the coming week. Ask the members to pray for the needs of one another during the week.

8. Conclude by praying aloud together the prayer at the end of one of the lessons discussed. You may choose to conclude the prayer by asking members to pray aloud any requests they may have.

"Brothers, I am a Pharisee, a son of Pharisees. I am on trial concerning the hope of the resurrection of the dead." Acts 23:6

Paul's Defense before the Council

ACTS 22:30–23:11 ³⁰*Since he wanted to find out what Paul was being accused of by the Jews, the next day he released him and ordered the chief priests and the entire council to meet. He brought Paul down and had him stand before them.*

23 ¹While Paul was looking intently at the council he said, "Brothers, up to this day I have lived my life with a clear conscience before God." ²Then the high priest Ananias ordered those standing near him to strike him on the mouth. ³At this Paul said to him, "God will strike you, you whitewashed wall! Are you sitting there to judge me according to the law, and yet in violation of the law you order me to be struck?" ⁴Those standing nearby said, "Do you dare to insult God's high priest?" ⁵And Paul said, "I did not realize, brothers, that he was high priest; for it is written, 'You shall not speak evil of a leader of your people.'"

⁶When Paul noticed that some were Sadducees and others were Pharisees, he called out in the council, "Brothers, I am a Pharisee, a son of Pharisees. I am on trial concerning the hope of the resurrection of the dead." ⁷When he said this, a dissension began between the Pharisees and the Sadducees, and the assembly was divided. ⁸(The Sadducees say that there is no resurrection, or angel, or spirit; but the Pharisees acknowledge all three.) [9]Then a great clamor arose, and certain scribes of the Pharisees' group stood up and contended, "We find nothing wrong with this man. What if a spirit or an angel has spoken to him?" [10]When the dissension became violent, the tribune, fearing that they would tear Paul to pieces, ordered the soldiers to go down, take him by force, and bring him into the barracks.

[11]That night the Lord stood near him and said, "Keep up your courage! For just as you have testified for me in Jerusalem, so you must bear witness also in Rome."

The remaining six chapters of Acts cover a period of about four years in Paul's life, during which Paul remains a prisoner in the custody of the Romans (24:27; 28:30). Yet despite his confinement, he continues to bear witness to Christ. In the same way that Luke has shown parallels to the passion of Jesus throughout Paul's journey to Jerusalem and his arrest, we see here echoes of Jesus' hearing before the Sanhedrin in the gospel (Luke 22:66) as Paul is brought before this same council of Jewish leaders in Jerusalem. The Roman tribune is determined to discover the reasons for the disturbances caused by the strong reactions to Paul. The prisoner stands before the Jewish council, unchained out of respect for his Roman citizenship, and addresses them.

Paul begins by asserting that he has always lived "with a clear conscience before God." He is claiming that his sincerity has always been equally real, both before and after his conversion experience. Paul has hardly begun his address when he is slapped by order of the high priest Ananias. The reigning high priest had a reputation for being quick-tempered and insolent, but such an act was allowed under the law only to defend God's honor against offense. Paul's response is a first-rate Jewish curse, calling the high priest a "whitewashed wall," a term denoting his hypocrisy. His clean surface appearance is a shallow cover for the insincerity and corruption within. Paul goes on to accuse Ananias of violating the law that he claims to defend, because Paul must be proven guilty with witnesses before being treated as a wrongdoer. When the other council members rebuke Paul for insulting the high priest, Paul responds that he did not know he was the high priest. This statement implies that the high priest's action was hardly the behavior expected of a person in that office. His actions against the law of Israel make him unrecogniz-able as the high priest.

Realizing that the Sanhedrin is composed of both Sadducees and Pharisees, Paul appeals to his own roots as a Pharisee (verse 6). One of the matters over which the two groups were divided was belief in the resurrection of the dead, which Pharisees accepted and Sadducees denied. Paul declares, "I am on trial concerning the hope of the resurrection of the dead." His words divert the assembly, dividing them over this central issue and disrupting their unified condemnation of him. In fact, some among the Pharisees declared him inno-cent, speculating that he could have had an experience of Jesus returned from death as an angel or a spirit (verse 9).

The resurrection of Jesus is the foundation of Paul's ministry, the heart of his mission. Although the Pharisees accept the resurrection as a future in which to hope, they resist Paul's testimony that the hoped-for resurrection has already begun in Jesus. This is the most fundamental issue dividing Paul from his opponents and separating Jewish followers of Jesus from all other Jews. Throughout the remainder of Acts, Paul will argue that the resurrection of Jesus from the dead is consistent with the most authentic beliefs of Judaism and the divine extension of Jewish hope. It is really the gospel that is on trial.

That night Paul experienced the risen Lord again. He tells Paul to take courage, and he promises that Paul will be his witness in Rome just as he has been in Jerusalem (verse 11). As uncertain and confused as things appear, God's plan is that Paul will go to Rome. The following sections of Acts—the plot on Paul's life, his transfer to Caesarea, and the progression of legal appeals—are all part of God's design that Paul bear witness to Christ in Rome.

Reflection and discussion

• How is Paul able to express his anger at the high priest's behavior yet also deeply respect the Torah and tradition of Israel? When have I felt something similar?

• What issues divide the Sadducees and the Pharisees? What issues divide me from other believers? Is there common ground on these issues, or is there an irreparable division?

• In what ways are the divisions between the Pharisees and Sadducees similar to the divisions among Christians today?

• What belief is at the center of my Christian faith? Where and how has God called me to bear witness for this belief?

Prayer

Lord Jesus, all the trials and unexpected turns in my life are part of your incomprehensible plan for me. Help me to remain courageous through life's challenges and to be your witness no matter what life brings my way.

"They have bound themselves by an oath neither to eat nor drink until they kill him. They are ready now and are waiting for your consent." Acts 23:21

The Plot to Kill Paul Uncovered

ACTS 23:12-22 *¹²In the morning the Jews joined in a conspiracy and bound themselves by an oath neither to eat nor drink until they had killed Paul. ¹³There were more than forty who joined in this conspiracy. ¹⁴They went to the chief priests and elders and said, "We have strictly bound ourselves by an oath to taste no food until we have killed Paul. ¹⁵Now then, you and the council must notify the tribune to bring him down to you, on the pretext that you want to make a more thorough examination of his case. And we are ready to do away with him before he arrives."*

¹⁶Now the son of Paul's sister heard about the ambush; so he went and gained entrance to the barracks and told Paul. ¹⁷Paul called one of the centurions and said, "Take this young man to the tribune, for he has something to report to him." ¹⁸So he took him, brought him to the tribune, and said, "The prisoner Paul called me and asked me to bring this young man to you; he has something to tell you." ¹⁹The tribune took him by the hand, drew him aside privately, and asked, "What is it that you have to report to me?" ²⁰He answered, "The Jews have agreed to ask you to bring Paul down to the council tomorrow, as though they were going to inquire more thoroughly into his case. ²¹But do not be persuaded by them, for more than forty of their men are lying in ambush for him. They have bound themselves by an oath neither to eat nor drink until they kill him.

They are ready now and are waiting for your consent." [22]So the tribune dismissed the young man, ordering him, "Tell no one that you have informed me of this."

The scene adds dramatic elements of suspense and intrigue to the saga of Paul in Jerusalem. The morning after Paul offered his testimony before the Jewish council in Jerusalem, a group of Jews decides to take matters into their own hands and put Paul to death. More than forty of them swear an oath among themselves to fast from food and drink until they kill Paul. The conspirators meet with the high priest and elders to involve them in their plot. They want the council to request to hear Paul again, to examine his case more thoroughly, in order to make a judgment for the tribune. But when Paul is on his way from the fortress to the Sanhedrin, the conspirators plan to seize him and put him to death.

In taking matters into their own hands, the plotters disregard the divine law they claim to be defending. They agree among themselves to lie and murder, a clear violation God's will as expressed in the Torah. The high priest's involvement in the conspiracy indicates the correctness of Paul's insult that he is a whitewashed wall. His deception and undercutting of the legal process is a great injustice and potentially will lead to homicide.

As it happens, the son of Paul's sister hears about the plot and comes to Paul with the story. Because of his status as a Roman citizen who is not yet convicted of a crime, Paul must have been allowed limited visitation from family. Paul then asks one of the centurions to take his nephew to the Roman commander to tell him about the danger. Paul's nephew reports the details of the conspiracy and how the forty assassins are ready to act if he agrees to another inquiry. As the tribune prepares to act, he tells the young man to let no one know that they have discussed the matter.

Luke underscores God's sovereign care for Paul throughout this saga. Through the plots and plans of enemies and friends, God is the unrecognized source of Paul's safety. In the face of great danger, the Roman tribune becomes Paul's unwitting protector. As the tribune prepares to act in response to this conspiracy, Paul will depart from Jerusalem for the last time and will be brought a step closer to his destiny in Rome. Through God's providence working behind the scenes, Paul will fulfill his divinely chosen mission, to bear witness to the Lord in Rome.

Reflection and discussion

• What might explain the fierce resolve of the forty conspirators to put Paul to death? What do they think they are trying to protect?

• In what sense is God's plan for Paul being worked out in the midst of the suspense and intrigue of this account?

• In the mystery of God's providence, often we cannot see why things happen as they do, yet God is at work in ways that we could not have planned for ourselves. When have I experienced this mystery?

Prayer

Lord, you are sovereign over all, and my life is in your hands. Even when life is perilous or my options limited, give me wisdom and freedom for serving you. When I do not see the way in front of me, let me know that you are guiding me.

"I found that he was accused concerning questions of their law, but was charged with nothing deserving death or imprisonment." Acts 23:29

Paul Sent to Felix in Caesarea

ACTS 23:23-35 *²³Then he summoned two of the centurions and said, "Get ready to leave by nine o'clock tonight for Caesarea with two hundred soldiers, seventy horsemen, and two hundred spearmen. ²⁴Also provide mounts for Paul to ride, and take him safely to Felix the governor." ²⁵He wrote a letter to this effect:*

²⁶"Claudius Lysias to his Excellency the governor Felix, greetings. ²⁷This man was seized by the Jews and was about to be killed by them, but when I had learned that he was a Roman citizen, I came with the guard and rescued him. ²⁸Since I wanted to know the charge for which they accused him, I had him brought to their council. ²⁹I found that he was accused concerning questions of their law, but was charged with nothing deserving death or imprisonment. ³⁰When I was informed that there would be a plot against the man, I sent him to you at once, ordering his accusers also to state before you what they have against him."

³¹So the soldiers, according to their instructions, took Paul and brought him during the night to Antipatris. ³²The next day they let the horsemen go on with him, while they returned to the barracks. ³³When they came to Caesarea and delivered the letter to the governor, they presented Paul also before him. [34]*On reading the letter, he asked what province he belonged to, and when he learned that he was from Cilicia,* [35]*he said, "I will give you a hearing when your accusers arrive." Then he ordered that he be kept under guard in Herod's headquarters.*

As soon as Paul's nephew departs from the fortress in Jerusalem where Paul is held, the tribune prepares to remove Paul under armed guard to Felix, the Roman governor in Caesarea. Because of the tension between the Jewish nationalists and their Roman occupiers, the large protective guard of soldiers and cavalry may not be unreasonable to escort Paul and shield him from ambush. Such displays of troops served as a reminder of Roman presence and their power to put down any rebellion. Taking advantage of the cover of darkness to leave Jerusalem for the last time, Paul will ride with the soldiers to Caesarea.

The Roman tribune, whose name is here revealed as Claudius Lysias, has written a letter explaining the case to be sent with the escort. The letter begins in the standard form, with the writer naming himself first, followed by a greeting of respect for Felix the governor (verse 26). Claudius then outlines the circumstances that brought Paul into his custody. He tweaks the truth in order to put the best possible face on his own conduct. As the previous narrative detailed, his actions with Paul from the beginning were not exactly a brave rescue of a Roman citizen.

Claudius had arrested Paul and was ready to interrogate him with scourging; only later did Paul reveal his Roman citizenship. Yet, to his credit, the tribune is now rescuing Paul from a conspiracy to have him killed. As far as he is concerned, Paul has done nothing worthy of imprisonment, much less of death (verse 29). All of his accusations involve questions related to the Jewish law, matters of internal Jewish debate and not issues that should concern the Roman courts. Believing that the governor was the proper authority to deal with the matter, the tribune has told the Jews that if they wish to bring charges they should do so before the governor.

The soldiers take Paul that night as far as Antipatris, which is on the road to Caesarea. Having completed the most dangerous part of the journey through the areas where an ambush could have been staged, the foot soldiers return to their barracks in Jerusalem while the horsemen continue on the way with Paul. The rest of the journey to Caesarea is through predominantly Gentile area, and so is less dangerous for Roman troops. When they arrive at Caesarea, the escort presents both the letter and the prisoner to the governor. When the governor discovers that Paul is from Cilicia, he could have sent Paul to be tried in his home province, but Felix decides to keep the case in Judea. He commits to a hearing when Paul's accusers arrive. Until then, Paul is held under guard in Herod's praetorium. Paul will spend two years here, where he is ironically under both the custody and protection of the Roman government.

Reflection and discussion

• Why is such a large protective escort necessary to accompany Paul to Caesarea? What does this indicate about the tensions between the Jewish population and the Roman forces?

• If the Roman tribune judges that Paul has done nothing worthy of imprisonment or death, why does he keep him under custody? How do these events enhance Paul's evangelizing mission?

Prayer

Providential God, you directed the events of Paul's life that he might be a witness to the gospel at the highest levels of the Roman Empire. Let me trust in your guidance and loving care through the events of my life.

"We have, in fact, found this man a pestilent fellow,
an agitator among all the Jews throughout the world,
and a ringleader of the sect of the Nazarenes." Acts 24:5

Paul Accused before Felix in Caesarea

ACTS 24:1-9 *¹Five days later the high priest Ananias came down with some elders and an attorney, a certain Tertullus, and they reported their case against Paul to the governor. ²When Paul had been summoned, Tertullus began to accuse him, saying: "Your Excellency, because of you we have long enjoyed peace, and reforms have been made for this people because of your foresight. ³We welcome this in every way and everywhere with utmost gratitude. ⁴But, to detain you no further, I beg you to hear us briefly with your customary graciousness. ⁵We have, in fact, found this man a pestilent fellow, an agitator among all the Jews throughout the world, and a ringleader of the sect of the Nazarenes. ⁶He even tried to profane the temple, and so we seized him. ⁸By examining him yourself you will be able to learn from him concerning everything of which we accuse him." ⁹The Jews also joined in the charge by asserting that all this was true.*

Within only five days of Paul's arrival in Caesarea, the high priest and elders of Jerusalem are ready to present their case against him. Perhaps they fear that Paul will be released unless they act quickly. They bring with them a professional advocate named Tertullus to speak for them. Latin was normally used in these courts, and such hired consultants were often employed by those who were themselves ignorant of the Roman law. As a professional orator, Tertullus tries to create a good presentation with very little substance to make his case.

Tertullus begins with a flurry of flattery for Felix. Yet, given what we know about how the Jewish leadership viewed him, the praise is not entirely sincere. The "peace" that Felix brought to the land refers to his suppression of the robber bands that had infested Judea, yet Tertullus does not refer to the ruthlessness with which he did it. Felix was a former slave, and with reference to this Tacitus remarked that "with savagery and lust he exercised the power of a king with the disposition of a slave." Before Felix's term as procurator began in AD 52, Jewish uprisings were isolated and infrequent, but they became epidemic by the end of his term in 58. His governorship is regarded as the turning point in the events that led up to the disastrous Jewish War in AD 66-70.

Tertullus states that he will not delay in getting to his point and presents the charges against Paul. First, he says that Paul is "a pestilent fellow." The word is, literally, "a plague," with the implication that he is deadly contagious. Second, Paul is called "an agitator among all the Jews throughout the world." Tertullus is trying to make Paul out to be one of the Jewish agitators who were appearing at the time, advocating revolution against Roman rule. Third, he says that Paul is "a ringleader of the sect of the Nazarenes." This indicates that Paul is an agitator among a new religious sect called the "Nazarenes," a disdainful way of referring to Christians. It designates followers of Jesus without including the messianic term Christ, and associates them with what many Jews saw as a false Messiah. Finally, Paul is charged with attempting "to profane the temple." This false charge, that Paul brought a Gentile into the sacred sanctuary, is the cause of the original disturbance (21:28).

These four accusations can be condensed to the accusation that Paul disturbs the civic peace as a subversive leader of a dangerous new sect. The high priest and the Jewish leaders join in agreement with these charges. These Jewish aristocrats were attempting to associate Paul and the Christian movement with the Jewish Zealots who were beginning to cause trouble for the Romans. Yet, the lack of evidence produced and the lack of any direct danger to Rome make it clear that the case against Paul is, at best, weak.

Reflection and discussion

• In what ways does Paul seem to be at a disadvantage as the delegation from Jerusalem comes to Caesarea to make their case against him?

• At this point, Felix only has the letter from Claudius Lysias (23:26-30) and the charges presented by Tertullus (verses 5-6). What might be his opinion of Paul?

• Felix was known for the way that he ruthlessly suppressed any public disorder or rebellion against Rome. How did Tertullus appeal to this characteristic of Felix in the way he presented the case against Paul?

Prayer

Lord God, the light of your gospel is often dimmed and obscured with misunderstandings and biased opinions. Lead me to see your saving truth with clarity and to witness your good news with transparency.

"But this I admit to you, that according to the Way, which they call a sect, I worship the God of our ancestors, believing everything laid down according to the law or written in the prophets." Acts 24:14

Paul's Defense and Captivity in Caesarea

ACTS 24:10-27 *¹⁰When the governor motioned to him to speak, Paul replied:*

"I cheerfully make my defense, knowing that for many years you have been a judge over this nation. ¹¹As you can find out, it is not more than twelve days since I went up to worship in Jerusalem. ¹²They did not find me disputing with anyone in the temple or stirring up a crowd either in the synagogues or through-out the city. ¹³Neither can they prove to you the charge that they now bring against me. ¹⁴But this I admit to you, that according to the Way, which they call a sect, I worship the God of our ancestors, believing everything laid down according to the law or written in the prophets. ¹⁵I have a hope in God—a hope that they themselves also accept—that there will be a resurrection of both the righteous and the unrighteous. ¹⁶Therefore I do my best always to have a clear conscience toward God and all people. ¹⁷Now after some years I came to bring alms to my nation and to offer sacrifices. ¹⁸While I was doing this, they found

me in the temple, completing the rite of purification, without any crowd or dis-
turbance. ¹⁹But there were some Jews from Asia—they ought to be here before
you to make an accusation, if they have anything against me. ²⁰Or let these men
here tell what crime they had found when I stood before the council, ²¹unless it
was this one sentence that I called out while standing before them, 'It is about
the resurrection of the dead that I am on trial before you today.'"

²²But Felix, who was rather well informed about the Way, adjourned the hear-
ing with the comment, "When Lysias the tribune comes down, I will decide your
case." ²³Then he ordered the centurion to keep him in custody, but to let him
have some liberty and not to prevent any of his friends from taking care of his
needs.

²⁴Some days later when Felix came with his wife Drusilla, who was Jewish, he
sent for Paul and heard him speak concerning faith in Christ Jesus. ²⁵And as he
discussed justice, self-control, and the coming judgment, Felix became frightened
and said, "Go away for the present; when I have an opportunity, I will send for
you." ²⁶At the same time he hoped that money would be given him by Paul, and
for that reason he used to send for him very often and converse with him.

²⁷After two years had passed, Felix was succeeded by Porcius Festus; and since
he wanted to grant the Jews a favor, Felix left Paul in prison.

Although Paul seems to be at a distinct disadvantage when compared to the Jewish leaders from Jerusalem with their professional advocate, he shows himself quite capable of offering his own defense. Paul expresses his appreciation for the opportunity to defend himself, implying that the governor will be able to discern the lack of evidence against him. He asserts his innocence by replying to each of the accusations against him.

First, Paul responds to the charge that he is a treacherous agitator (verses 11-13). His coming to Jerusalem twelve days ago was to worship God. He flatly denies disputing with anyone or stirring up a crowd, either in the temple, the synagogues, or the city. His accusers are unable to present any evidence of their allegations.

Next, Paul answers the charge that he is a leader of the deviant Nazarene sect (verses 14-16). Although there was a time before his conversion when Paul had shared his accusers' opinion of "the Way," he now understands it, not as a deviation from Judaism, but as its fullest expression. He remains a loyal

Jew, still worshiping "the God of our ancestors." He believes everything written in the Torah and the prophets. This ancient faith leads to hope in God, to trust in God's final deliverance through the resurrection of the dead. Thus, Paul affirms with a clear conscience that God's way to salvation is rooted in old promises and that, far from leading a subversive movement, he is a good and faithful Jew.

Finally, Paul deals with the charge of profaning the temple (verses 17-19). He says that he returned to Jerusalem after some years of travel to present to the Jewish Christians a monetary offering he had collected among the believers throughout the empire. He also returned to offer a sacrifice of thanksgiving to God in the temple. During his rite of purification, he was accused by some Jews from the province of Asia of desecrating the holy place. Paul says that his accusers ought to be present if they have a charge against him.

Paul demands that the religious leaders of Jerusalem, who have already heard his case in the Sanhedrin, should state what crime they found in him. There has already been an examination of the facts, and Paul says that the leaders can testify that he has done nothing worthy of punishment. Paul declares that they have established only "one sentence"—that he believes in the resurrection: "It is about the resurrection of the dead that I am on trial before you today" (verse 21).

Since Felix is rather well informed about the Way, and since he seems to understand that the Way is no threat to the Roman order, he decides to delay his decision, pending further consultation with the tribune. So he simply adjourns the case, leaving Paul with no choice but to wait and hope for discharge. Although he remained a prisoner, Paul is granted the freedom to be visited and cared for by friends. Even Felix and his Jewish wife Drusilla would visit and converse with him in private, as Paul spoke to them about "faith in Christ Jesus" (verse 24).

But, understanding that Felix was a corrupt and cruel procurator, it is no wonder that he became frightened and dismissed Paul when he began to speak about "justice, self-control, and the coming judgment" (verses 24-25). Felix kept Paul in custody for two years, hoping to receive a bribe from Paul and seeking to satisfy the leaders in Jerusalem. And although his captivity prevented Paul from bringing the gospel to new lands as he wished, we can be assured that Paul made the best of his situation by witnessing to Jesus Christ even in prison.

Reflection and discussion

• Paul was prevented from doing what he wanted to do and what he thought he ought to do. What does he teach me through how he made the best of his situation?

• When have I been misunderstood or falsely accused by others because of my beliefs? What have I learned about being a witness for Christ in such difficult situations?

• Luke tells us that Felix was "rather well informed about the Way," but he was clearly not a believer. What is the difference between being well informed about the church of Jesus Christ and being a disciple of him?

Prayer

God of our ancestors, you have called men and women to follow your way throughout the ages. Help me to realize that I belong to a great company of witnesses, and teach me what to say and do for you.

"I am appealing to the emperor's tribunal; this is where I should be tried. I have done no wrong to the Jews, as you very well know." Acts 25:10

Paul Appeals His Case to the Emperor

ACTS 25:1-12 *¹Three days after Festus had arrived in the province, he went up from Caesarea to Jerusalem ²where the chief priests and the leaders of the Jews gave him a report against Paul. They appealed to him ³and requested, as a favor to them against Paul, to have him transferred to Jerusalem. They were, in fact, planning an ambush to kill him along the way. ⁴Festus replied that Paul was being kept at Caesarea, and that he himself intended to go there shortly. ⁵"So," he said, "let those of you who have the authority come down with me, and if there is anything wrong about the man, let them accuse him." ⁶After he had stayed among them not more than eight or ten days, he went down to Caesarea; the next day he took his seat on the tribunal and ordered Paul to be brought. ⁷When he arrived, the Jews who had gone down from Jerusalem surrounded him, bringing many serious charges against him, which they could not prove. ⁸Paul said in his defense, "I have in no way committed an offense against the law of the Jews, or against the temple, or against the emperor." ⁹But Festus, wishing to do the Jews a favor, asked Paul, "Do you wish to go up to Jerusalem and be tried there before me on these charges?" ¹⁰Paul said, "I am appealing to the emperor's tribunal; this is where I should be tried. I have done no wrong to the Jews, as you very well know. ¹¹Now if I am in the wrong and have committed* *something for which I deserve to die, I am not trying to escape death; but if there is nothing to their charges against me, no one can turn me over to them. I appeal to the emperor." ¹²Then Festus, after he had conferred with his council, replied, "You have appealed to the emperor; to the emperor you will go."*

Two years have passed and Paul is still in prison at Caesarea. The new procurator of Judea, Porcius Festus, has succeeded Antonius Felix. Within three days of his arrival in Caesarea, Festus paid a courtesy visit to the Jewish capital. It was important for the new governor to establish a working relationship with the high priest and the Sanhedrin as soon as possible to keep peace and order. Even after all this time, Paul's enemies are still intent on killing him. They try to convince the new Roman governor to send Paul to Jerusalem for a retrial, but they are planning to ambush and assassinate him along the way (verse 3).

In reply, Festus says that Paul is in Caesarea and will be examined there upon his return. If Paul has done anything legally wrong, the Jewish authorities should return with him and accuse him in Caesarea. By requiring that Paul be tried in Caesarea for strictly pragmatic reasons, Festus unknowingly protects him and saves him from death.

When Festus returns to Caesarea, he convenes a hearing the next day and orders that Paul be brought to him. The Jews from Jerusalem have come to the city, and they accuse Paul of many serious crimes. Yet, Luke tells us that they cannot prove their charges. In his own defense, Paul states that he has not committed any legal offense, breaking neither the Jewish laws of the temple nor the Roman laws of the emperor (verse 8). He is both a faithful Jew and a good citizen.

Still trying to win the favor of the Jews, Festus asks Paul if he wishes to be tried in Jerusalem. Paul knows that a return to Jerusalem would bring almost certain death, either through an unjust guilty verdict in a trial or his assassination on the way. But, in this political game being played between the Roman and Jewish leaders, Paul has a trump card. Because he is a Roman citizen, he can have his case transferred to a Roman court for trial. So, in response to Festus' question, Paul states, "I am appealing to the emperor's tribunal; this is where I should be tried" (verse 10). By playing this card, Paul removes his case from both the Jewish leaders and the Roman governor.

Paul's "appeal to the emperor" is rooted in one of the oldest rights of Roman citizens. It does not endear him to Festus because it calls into question his impartiality as a judge. Yet, Festus approves the appeal, thereby withdrawing his own responsibility for the case and ridding himself of a perplexing dilemma. "You have appealed to the emperor," Festus declares, "to the emperor you will go." The Roman emperor at the time is Nero, whose early reign was relatively tranquil, but whose later days will see grim days for the Christians of Rome.

Paul's final movement to Rome can now proceed. Once again, God's providence is protecting Paul by means of Roman law, and Luke is demonstrating that the Christian faith is not a threat to the peace of any civil state. By appealing his case to Rome, Paul is in a sense sending himself there. His greatest concern is taking the gospel there, knowing that God desires him to bear witness in Rome before his death (23:11).

Reflection and discussion

• What convinces me most from Paul's legal defense that he is both a faithful Jew and a good citizen of the empire?

• What do you find most inspiring or motivating about the travels, adventures, and speeches of Paul?

Prayer

Lord God, your sovereign will directed the events and decisions of Paul's life so that the good news was brought to the world. Teach me how to trust in your guidance and to use the opportunities that come my way for the sake of your kingdom.

SUGGESTIONS FOR FACILITATORS, GROUP SESSION 5

1. Welcome group members and ask if anyone has any questions, announcements, or requests.

2. You may want to pray this prayer as a group:

> *Providential God, you directed the travels, speeches, and adventures of Paul so that he became the instrument of your kingdom that you desired him to be. As your apostle to the Gentiles, he traveled throughout the empire and witnessed to the gospel from Jerusalem to Rome. Teach us how to entrust our lives to you, so that you can direct our ways and allow us to serve you as you wish. Show us how to take advantage of the opportunities you have placed before us and to respond with courage to your call to be witnesses of the gospel in our world.*

3. Ask one or more of the following questions:
   - What most intrigued you from this week's study?
   - What makes you want to know and understand more of God's word?

4. Discuss lessons 19 through 24. Choose one or more of the questions for reflection and discussion from each lesson to talk over as a group.

5. Ask the group members to name one thing they have most appreciated about the way the group has worked during this Bible study. Ask group members to discuss any changes they might suggest in the way the group works in future studies.

6. Invite group members to complete lessons 25 through 30 on their own during the six days before the next meeting. They should write out their own answers to the questions as preparation for next week's session.

7. Ask group members what they find most fascinating about Paul in the Acts of the Apostles. Discuss some of these insights in Luke's presentation of Paul.

8. Conclude by praying aloud together the prayer at the end of one of the lessons discussed. You may want to conclude the prayer by asking members to voice prayers of thanksgiving.

"I found that he had done nothing deserving death; and when he appealed to his Imperial Majesty, I decided to send him. But I have nothing definite to write to our sovereign about him." Acts 25:25-26

Paul's Defense before King Agrippa

ACTS 25:13–26:11 *¹³After several days had passed, King Agrippa and Bernice arrived at Caesarea to welcome Festus. ¹⁴Since they were staying there several days, Festus laid Paul's case before the king, saying, "There is a man here who was left in prison by Felix. ¹⁵When I was in Jerusalem, the chief priests and the elders of the Jews informed me about him and asked for a sentence against him. ¹⁶I told them that it was not the custom of the Romans to hand over anyone before the accused had met the accusers face to face and had been given an opportunity to make a defense against the charge. ¹⁷So when they met here, I lost no time, but on the next day took my seat on the tribunal and ordered the man to be brought. ¹⁸When the accusers stood up, they did not charge him with any of the crimes that I was expecting. ¹⁹Instead they had certain points of disagreement with him about their own religion and about a certain Jesus, who had died, but whom Paul asserted to be alive. ²⁰Since I was at a loss how to investigate these questions, I asked whether he wished to go to Jerusalem and be tried there on these charges. ²¹But when Paul had appealed to be kept in custody for* the decision of his Imperial Majesty, I ordered him to be held until I could send him to the emperor." [22]Agrippa said to Festus, "I would like to hear the man myself." "Tomorrow," he said, "you will hear him."

[23]So on the next day Agrippa and Bernice came with great pomp, and they entered the audience hall with the military tribunes and the prominent men of the city. Then Festus gave the order and Paul was brought in. [24]And Festus said, "King Agrippa and all here present with us, you see this man about whom the whole Jewish community petitioned me, both in Jerusalem and here, shouting that he ought not to live any longer. [25]But I found that he had done nothing deserving death; and when he appealed to his Imperial Majesty, I decided to send him. [26]But I have nothing definite to write to our sovereign about him. Therefore I have brought him before all of you, and especially before you, King Agrippa, so that, after we have examined him, I may have something to write— [27]for it seems to me unreasonable to send a prisoner without indicating the charges against him."

26 [1]Agrippa said to Paul, "You have permission to speak for yourself." Then Paul stretched out his hand and began to defend himself:

[2]"I consider myself fortunate that it is before you, King Agrippa, I am to make my defense today against all the accusations of the Jews, [3]because you are especially familiar with all the customs and controversies of the Jews; therefore I beg of you to listen to me patiently.

[4]"All the Jews know my way of life from my youth, a life spent from the beginning among my own people and in Jerusalem. [5]They have known for a long time, if they are willing to testify, that I have belonged to the strictest sect of our religion and lived as a Pharisee. [6]And now I stand here on trial on account of my hope in the promise made by God to our ancestors, [7]a promise that our twelve tribes hope to attain, as they earnestly worship day and night. It is for this hope, your Excellency, that I am accused by Jews! [8]Why is it thought incredible by any of you that God raises the dead?

[9]"Indeed, I myself was convinced that I ought to do many things against the name of Jesus of Nazareth. [10]And that is what I did in Jerusalem; with authority received from the chief priests, I not only locked up many of the saints in prison, but I also cast my vote against them when they were being condemned to death. [11]By punishing them often in all the synagogues I tried to force them to blaspheme; and since I was so furiously enraged at them, I pursued them even to foreign cities.

P aul's appeal of his case to the emperor presents a predicament to Festus, who must now send a report along with Paul to Rome explaining the charges on which he is to be tried. The opportunity for Festus to seek help with his quandary arises when King Agrippa arrives in Caesarea for a state visit to pay respect to Festus, the new Roman governor. Agrippa is the great-grandson of Herod the Great, ruler of the region at Jesus' birth. He is accompanied by Bernice, his sister, who lives in the palace with him. Agrippa is part Jewish and has been given by the emperor the right to appoint the high priests and protect the sacred vestments. Agrippa is therefore someone to whom Festus could turn for an informed opinion on matters related to the Jewish religion.

Festus reviews the situation with Agrippa. He notes that the Jewish chief priests and elders wanted a judgment against Paul, but he insisted that Paul have an opportunity to defend himself before his accusers. Festus explains that he brought Paul to trial with no delays, but he was surprised that his accusers did not charge him with crimes as he had expected (verse 18). Rather, Festus found himself dealing with religious disputes, not matters of civil law. Specifically, the issue is "about a certain Jesus, who had died, but whom Paul asserted to be alive" (verse 19). Festus states that he offered Paul the opportunity to be tried in Jerusalem by the Jews, but Paul appealed his case to the emperor. So Festus reports that he is keeping Paul until he can be sent to Rome, but first he must get what information he can for the dossier that would accompany the prisoner. When Agrippa asks to hear Paul's case, Festus agrees that he will do so the very next day.

The audience takes place with great pomp, with King Agrippa and Bernice accompanied by a distinguished audience of high-ranking officers and leading men of the city. In contrast, Paul stands before them, chained and in simple garb. The occasion is not a trial; at best it is an informal hearing and perhaps a form of entertainment. The royal couple plays for Festus the same role that King Herod played for Pilate in the trial of Jesus (Luke 23:6-12). The Roman governors, first Pilate and later Festus, recognize the importance of the Jewish kings, first Herod and later Agrippa, and show them deference. Once again, the passion of Paul resembles that of Jesus. Paul's examination fulfills the prophecy Jesus gave to his disciples, "You will be brought before kings and governors because of my name" (Luke 21:12). Festus, like Pilate with Jesus, admits that he has found no crime in Paul deserving death (verse 25).

Paul's speech before Agrippa, Bernice, and Festus is his last major discourse in Acts. Elements of his earlier defenses carry over to this one. Paul sets forth his life story, emphasizing that he has always been a Jew, growing up in Jerusalem and following the strict ways of the Pharisees. He states, "I stand here on trial on account of my hope in the promise made by God to our ancestors" (26:6). In his defense, Paul explains that his faith does not violate the heritage of Israel. The roots of this new faith are in fact old, fulfilling God's ancient promises to his people. Because Paul at first perceived faith in Jesus as a threat to the traditions of Israel, he pursued and punished believers and put them to death. But in fact he has come to understand that the resurrection of the dead, the centerpiece of his preaching, is the essence of Jewish hope.

Reflection and discussion

• Why does Festus consult with Agrippa about Paul's case? Why might Agrippa want to meet Paul and hear what he has to say?

• In the midst of his trials, Paul found ways to witness to Jesus Christ. What might be some ways that I could bear witness to him in the midst of life's struggles and tribulations?

Prayer

Suffering Lord, your servant Paul responded to his trials by finding ways to serve you. Teach me to use the difficult ordeals of my life as an opportunity to grow in your crucified image. May I witness to your life within me even in life's most difficult situations.

"King Agrippa, do you believe the prophets? I know that you believe."
Agrippa said to Paul, "Are you so quickly persuading me
to become a Christian?" Acts 26:27-28

King Agrippa Responds to Paul

ACTS 26:12-32 *¹²"With this in mind, I was traveling to Damascus with the authority and commission of the chief priests, ¹³when at midday along the road, your Excellency, I saw a light from heaven, brighter than the sun, shining around me and my companions. ¹⁴When we had all fallen to the ground, I heard a voice saying to me in the Hebrew language, 'Saul, Saul, why are you persecuting me? It hurts you to kick against the goads.' ¹⁵I asked, 'Who are you, Lord?' The Lord answered, 'I am Jesus whom you are persecuting. ¹⁶But get up and stand on your feet; for I have appeared to you for this purpose, to appoint you to serve and testify to the things in which you have seen me and to those in which I will appear to you. ¹⁷I will rescue you from your people and from the Gentiles—to whom I am sending you ¹⁸to open their eyes so that they may turn from darkness to light and from the power of Satan to God, so that they may receive forgiveness of sins and a place among those who are sanctified by faith in me.'*

¹⁹"After that, King Agrippa, I was not disobedient to the heavenly vision, ²⁰but declared first to those in Damascus, then in Jerusalem and throughout the countryside of Judea, and also to the Gentiles, that they should repent and turn to God and do deeds consistent with repentance. ²¹For this reason the Jews seized me in the temple and tried to kill me. ²²To this day I have had help from God, and so I stand here, testifying to both small and great, saying nothing but what the prophets and Moses said would take place: ²³that the Messiah must suffer, and that, by being the first to rise from the dead, he would proclaim light both to our people and to the Gentiles."

²⁴While he was making this defense, Festus exclaimed, "You are out of your mind, Paul! Too much learning is driving you insane!" ²⁵But Paul said, "I am not out of my mind, most excellent Festus, but I am speaking the sober truth. ²⁶Indeed the king knows about these things, and to him I speak freely; for I am certain that none of these things has escaped his notice, for this was not done in a corner. ²⁷King Agrippa, do you believe the prophets? I know that you believe." ²⁸Agrippa said to Paul, "Are you so quickly persuading me to become a Christian?" ²⁹Paul replied, "Whether quickly or not, I pray to God that not only you but also all who are listening to me today might become such as I am— except for these chains."

³⁰Then the king got up, and with him the governor and Bernice and those who had been seated with them; ³¹and as they were leaving, they said to one another, "This man is doing nothing to deserve death or imprisonment." ³²Agrippa said to Festus, "This man could have been set free if he had not appealed to the emperor."

Paul's last major discourse is a defense of his life's mission. Once more we hear Paul's account of his experience of the Risen Lord on the road to Damascus, the third telling in Acts. Each narrative offers additional aspects of what took place and different facets of its meaning. Here Paul emphasizes light and sight as his symbolic themes. He recounts that he saw "a light from heaven, brighter than the sun." Yet, here there is no mention of Paul's own loss of sight. Instead, the image of blindness is applied to the Gentiles to whom Paul is sent. His mission is "to open their eyes so that they may turn from darkness to light" (verse 18). This turning to see the light expresses a personal turning from sin and Satan's power to the forgiveness and sanctification offered through faith in the Risen Christ.

From the beginning of his gospel to the end of Acts, Luke has expressed the good news of the Messiah through images of light from the prophet Isaiah. During Jesus' presentation in the temple as an infant, Simeon spoke: "My eyes have seen your salvation" (Isa 40:5), "a light of revelation to the Gentiles" (Isa 42:6; 49:6). When Paul and Barnabas turned to the Gentiles, they state the Lord's command to them in the words of Isaiah: "I have set you to be a light for the Gentiles, so that you may bring salvation to the ends of the earth" (Acts 13:47). Here Paul's summary of his mission—bringing the light of salvation to the Gentiles—indicates that what Paul is doing is not only in continuity with the mission of Jesus, but is even the work of the risen Lord himself. Then, at the end of Acts, Paul again uses words from Isaiah to characterize those who fail to respond to the gospel of salvation: "They have shut their eyes, so that they might not look with their eyes" (Isa 6:10; Acts 28:27). The people of Israel who refuse to believe are as blind as Paul before his conversion.

Paul's testimony is centered on the scandalous assertion of the crucified Messiah who has been raised from the dead, proclaiming light to both Jews and Gentiles (verse 23). Yet, he claims that his witness is nothing new; rather, it is "what the prophets and Moses said would take place" (verse 22). The gospel Paul proclaims is nothing more than the fulfillment of the ancient hopes of Israel. The suffering Messiah, the resurrection from the dead, and salvation to all people, Jews and Gentiles alike, is the path set forth throughout the Torah and prophets of Israel. Faith in Jesus is thoroughly Jewish, yet it is destined for all the world to hear and believe. It is the completion of God's plan to redeem the whole world and bring divine blessings to all.

Although Paul is defending himself, he is also witnessing his faith to Festus, Agrippa, Bernice, and all who are listening. He wants them to experience the forgiveness and life God is offering them through faith in Christ. When Festus proclaims that Paul has lost his mind, Paul addresses him respectfully, stating that he has control of his thoughts and speaks the truth (verse 25). As Paul addresses Agrippa, the king quips that Paul may persuade him "to become a Christian" (verse 28). This is the second and final time the term "Christian" is used in Acts (see 11:26). Agrippa's joke leads Paul to express his deepest hope: "I pray to God that not only you but also all who are listening to me today might become such as I am" (verse 29).

Paul's hearers declare that he has done nothing that deserves death or imprisonment. Like Jesus, he has been declared innocent three times by Roman officials and a Jewish king: Lysias (23:29), Festus (25:25), and now King Agrippa. But Paul's appeal to Caesar requires that he remain imprisoned. So to Rome he must go to fulfill his destiny.

Reflection and discussion

• Paul uses the images of "opening eyes" and "turning to the light" as a metaphor for faith. In what ways is the experience of faith like seeing the light?

• The personal nature of Paul's testimony is part of what makes his message so powerful and effective. When has the personal testimony of another awakened or deepened faith in me?

• How would I respond if put on trial for being a Christian? Would there be sufficient evidence to convict me?

Prayer

Risen Lord, you have made yourself known to me that I may be your witness to others. Help me to do my part in witnessing to you so that others may come to believe. Show me how to be an instrument of your forgiveness and salvation for others.

"Sirs, I can see that the voyage will be with danger and much heavy loss, not only of the cargo and the ship, but also of our lives." Acts 27:10

Paul Sets Sail for Rome

ACTS 27:1-12 *¹When it was decided that we were to sail for Italy, they transferred Paul and some other prisoners to a centurion of the Augustan Cohort, named Julius. ²Embarking on a ship of Adramyttium that was about to set sail to the ports along the coast of Asia, we put to sea, accompanied by Aristarchus, a Macedonian from Thessalonica. ³The next day we put in at Sidon; and Julius treated Paul kindly, and allowed him to go to his friends to be cared for. ⁴Putting out to sea from there, we sailed under the lee of Cyprus, because the winds were against us. ⁵After we had sailed across the sea that is off Cilicia and Pamphylia, we came to Myra in Lycia. ⁶There the centurion found an Alexandrian ship bound for Italy and put us on board. ⁷We sailed slowly for a number of days and arrived with difficulty off Cnidus, and as the wind was against us, we sailed under the lee of Crete off Salmone. ⁸Sailing past it with difficulty, we came to a place called Fair Havens, near the city of Lasea.*

⁹Since much time had been lost and sailing was now dangerous, because even the Fast had already gone by, Paul advised them, ¹⁰saying, "Sirs, I can see that the voyage will be with danger and much heavy loss, not only of the cargo and the ship, but also of our lives." ¹¹But the centurion paid more attention to the pilot and to the owner of the ship than to what Paul said.

¹²Since the harbor was not suitable for spending the winter, the majority was in favor of putting to sea from there, on the chance that somehow they could reach Phoenix, where they could spend the winter. It was a harbor of Crete, facing southwest and northwest.

Voyages on the seas were rare in the literature of ancient Israel. The sea was associated with the powers of chaos, and the book of Jonah demonstrates the terrible things that can happen to those who travel by sea. In contrast, accounts of sea voyages, storms, and shipwrecks were common in Greek and Roman literature. Paul had to travel often by sea if he was to bring the gospel to the ends of the earth. He reports in his letters that peril on the sea was among his trials: "Three times I was shipwrecked; for a night and a day I was adrift at sea" (2 Cor 11:25).

The Roman authorities have decided to send Paul and other prisoners to Italy, and then from the Italian port to the city of Rome. Luke's description of the voyage has the feel and details of an eyewitness account. The fact that the "we" passages reappear here is a good indication that the voyage was made in the company of the author himself. Luke describes the adventure as a master storyteller in a way that serves his account of what God accomplishes in these events. The detailed and difficult voyage is designed to show God's determination to bring Paul to Rome.

The prisoners were put in the charge of an escort under the command of a centurion named Julius. He secured passage for his charges on a ship bound for the Aegean region. After departing from Caesarea, they would sail along the ports of the province of Asia. Their first port of call is Sidon, an ancient city that has a Christian community that is evidently known to Paul. The centurion allows Paul the unusual liberty of visiting the community ashore. Although Paul would have been accompanied by soldiers, their permitting the visit indicates that he was not seen as a security risk. Paul is cared for by his friends there, and he may very well have picked up food and supplies for the journey (verse 3).

Putting out to sea again, the ship sails to the north of Cyprus to gain some shelter from the winds and to take advantage of the westward currents running along the coast. Their next stop is Myra. Here the centurion finds a ship bound for Italy and transfers the prisoners to it. Then with difficulty they make their way westward until they reach a point off Cnidus. Beyond this point, they would no longer be protected by the land. But they choose to go on, confident of reaching Italy before the close of the sailing season. Unable to continue westward because of the winds, they head south to sail under the shelter of Crete. They eventually land at a harbor named Fair Havens on the south coast of Crete.

Since it is already late in the year, sailing is becoming increasingly more dangerous. During the stormy months, beginning in November, shipping in the Mediterranean was closed. Ships' captains took their vessels into harbor and waited for the return of fair weather in the spring. Mention of "the Fast" refers to the Jewish Day of Atonement (verse 9). Luke's mention that this feast has already past puts the time probably around mid-October. Although Festus had accused Paul of being out of his mind, Paul seems to have a good supply of practical sense here. He warns that leaving the harbor will result in a heavy loss of cargo and ship, and even lives (verse 10). But the advice of the pilot and the ship owner prevails. They press on with the goal of reaching Phoenix, a more secure harbor of Crete, where they could pass the winter.

Reflection and discussion

• Consult a map and locate the places where Paul traveled by ship. How do these Roman provinces correspond to the countries of today?

• Count how many times Luke uses the pronoun "we" in describing these scenes. In what ways does the use of "we" suggest the historical details of an eyewitness to the events?

• If I were to describe my life as a weather report, what are today's conditions? What is the future forecast?

•Despite the fact that God is not mentioned in this narrative, the presence of God is felt throughout. How is God's providence evident in these events?

• In the early church, the ship became an image of the church in Christian art and literature. Why is the ship an especially effective image of Christ's church?

Prayer

Lord and Master, you guide my life's journey through calm waters and stormy seas. Assure me of your protective presence with me, and lead me through the trials and sufferings of this life to the fair haven of your heavenly kingdom.

"Do not be afraid, Paul; you must stand before the emperor; and indeed, God has granted safety to all those who are sailing with you." Acts 27:24

Storm at Sea and Shipwreck

ACTS 27:13-44 *¹³When a moderate south wind began to blow, they thought they could achieve their purpose; so they weighed anchor and began to sail past Crete, close to the shore. ¹⁴But soon a violent wind, called the northeaster, rushed down from Crete. ¹⁵Since the ship was caught and could not be turned head-on into the wind, we gave way to it and were driven. ¹⁶By running under the lee of a small island called Cauda we were scarcely able to get the ship's boat under control. ¹⁷After hoisting it up they took measures to undergird the ship; then, fearing that they would run on the Syrtis, they lowered the sea anchor and so were driven. ¹⁸We were being pounded by the storm so violently that on the next day they began to throw the cargo overboard, ¹⁹and on the third day with their own hands they threw the ship's tackle overboard. ²⁰When neither sun nor stars appeared for many days, and no small tempest raged, all hope of our being saved was at last abandoned.*

²¹Since they had been without food for a long time, Paul then stood up among them and said, "Men, you should have listened to me and not have set sail from Crete and thereby avoided this damage and loss. ²²I urge you now to keep up your courage, for there will be no loss of life among you, but only of the ship. ^{23}*For last night there stood by me an angel of the God to whom I belong and whom I worship,* ^{24}*and he said, 'Do not be afraid, Paul; you must stand before the emperor; and indeed, God has granted safety to all those who are sailing with you.'* ^{25}*So keep up your courage, men, for I have faith in God that it will be exactly as I have been told.* ^{26}*But we will have to run aground on some island."*

^{27}*When the fourteenth night had come, as we were drifting across the sea of Adria, about midnight the sailors suspected that they were nearing land.* ^{28}*So they took soundings and found twenty fathoms; a little farther on they took soundings again and found fifteen fathoms.* ^{29}*Fearing that we might run on the rocks, they let down four anchors from the stern and prayed for day to come.* ^{30}*But when the sailors tried to escape from the ship and had lowered the boat into the sea, on the pretext of putting out anchors from the bow,* ^{31}*Paul said to the centurion and the soldiers, "Unless these men stay in the ship, you cannot be saved."* ^{32}*Then the soldiers cut away the ropes of the boat and set it adrift.*

^{33}*Just before daybreak, Paul urged all of them to take some food, saying, "Today is the fourteenth day that you have been in suspense and remaining without food, having eaten nothing.* ^{34}*Therefore I urge you to take some food, for it will help you survive; for none of you will lose a hair from your heads."* ^{35}*After he had said this, he took bread; and giving thanks to God in the presence of all, he broke it and began to eat.* ^{36}*Then all of them were encouraged and took food for themselves.* ^{37}*(We were in all two hundred seventy-six persons in the ship.)* ^{38}*After they had satisfied their hunger, they lightened the ship by throwing the wheat into the sea.*

^{39}*In the morning they did not recognize the land, but they noticed a bay with a beach, on which they planned to run the ship ashore, if they could.* ^{40}*So they cast off the anchors and left them in the sea. At the same time they loosened the ropes that tied the steering-oars; then hoisting the foresail to the wind, they made for the beach.* ^{41}*But striking a reef, they ran the ship aground; the bow stuck and remained immovable, but the stern was being broken up by the force of the waves.* ^{42}*The soldiers' plan was to kill the prisoners, so that none might swim away and escape;* ^{43}*but the centurion, wishing to save Paul, kept them from carrying out their plan. He ordered those who could swim to jump overboard first and make for the land,* ^{44}*and the rest to follow, some on planks and others on pieces of the ship. And so it was that all were brought safely to land.*

Although the ship begins sailing westward with a south breeze, suddenly the winds shift and a severe windstorm sweeps down from the mountains of Crete from the northeast. Unable to face the wind, the crew is incapable of controlling the ship and they are driven southward. Making what preparations they can for surviving the storm, they shorten the sail, bring the lifeboat on board, and undergird the ship with ropes to ensure that the timber hull stays together. They fear hitting the Syrtis, a group of shallow gulfs full of treacherous rocks and sandbanks on the northern coast of Africa. They lower the sea anchor to create drag and begin to toss the cargo and gear overboard in order to let the ship sit higher on the sea so they will take in less water. Unable to see the sun or the stars for many days, they are incapable of estimating their locations or even their direction. As one day stretches into another while the storm rages around them, they lose all hope of being saved.

Paul stands amid the passengers and crew of the ship to encourage them. Reminding them of his advice not to set sail because of the danger and potential of loss, he appeals now to be heard as a credible speaker. In the midst of their great danger, Paul assures the passengers and crew that there will be no loss of life among them, but only the ship will be lost. He explains that God's angel had spoken to him during the night to reveal God's plan. The vision confirmed that Paul must stand before the emperor in Rome, and that God pledges to grant safety to all who are sailing with him.

About midnight on the fourteenth night at sea since leaving Fair Havens, the seamen detect signs of approaching land. Fearing that they might run aground, they drop anchors, hoping that the morning light will reveal their location. It seems that the crew has come to trust Paul. He warns that they will remain safe only if they stay with the ship. As the apostles had experienced the protective presence of Jesus when they were caught in storms on the Sea of Galilee, now Paul has been assured of God's protection on the high seas of the Mediterranean. Paul reiterates the proverbial saying Jesus had used to reassure his disciples: "none of you will lose a hair from your heads" (verse 34; Luke 21:18). Then Paul urges the passengers to take some food so that they will survive. He takes bread and repeats the eucharistic actions of Jesus: giving thanks, breaking it, and eating (verse 35; Luke 22:19: 24:30). Luke's Christian readers would not fail to catch the allusion to the Eucharist here. In the midst of great danger, Paul has offered the saving presence of Jesus to all in the ship.

God is delivering them as he had told Paul that he would. The number of people on board the ship is given at two hundred seventy-six, underlining the marvel that they will all be saved. Through Paul, as through Jesus, God has delivered all who were in peril and danger of death.

The place where the ship ran aground is what is today called Saint Paul's Bay at the island of Malta. The bow of the ship becomes stuck at a shallow place, and the stern is breaking by the impact and the pounding waves. The soldiers want to kill the prisoners since they will be liable for allowing them to escape. But the centurion will not allow the execution because he wants to save Paul. He orders everyone to get ashore as best they can—first those who could swim, then the others by floating on planks or broken pieces of the ship. Through God's protection, all reach land safely.

Reflection and discussion

• In what ways does Paul stand out from the other passengers of the ship in these scenes? How was he able to offer hope and confidence to the others during times of crisis?

• How do I balance natural fears and supernatural trust when I am faced with worries and danger?

Prayer

Lord Jesus, you are with me even in the worst of storms. Calm my fears and help me to trust in your protection and your power to save me. Through faith and Eucharist, give me strength and lead me through threat and peril.

And so we came to Rome. The believers from there, when they heard of us,
came as far as the Forum of Appius and Three Taverns to meet us.
On seeing them, Paul thanked God and took courage. Acts 28:14-15

From the Island of Malta to Rome

ACTS 28:1-16 *¹After we had reached safety, we then learned that the island was called Malta. ²The natives showed us unusual kindness. Since it had begun to rain and was cold, they kindled a fire and welcomed all of us around it. ³Paul had gathered a bundle of brushwood and was putting it on the fire, when a viper, driven out by the heat, fastened itself on his hand. ⁴When the natives saw the creature hanging from his hand, they said to one another, "This man must be a murderer; though he has escaped from the sea, justice has not allowed him to live." ⁵He, however, shook off the creature into the fire and suffered no harm. ⁶They were expecting him to swell up or drop dead, but after they had waited a long time and saw that nothing unusual had happened to him, they changed their minds and began to say that he was a god.*

⁷Now in the neighborhood of that place were lands belonging to the leading man of the island, named Publius, who received us and entertained us hospitably for three days. ⁸It so happened that the father of Publius lay sick in bed with fever and dysentery. Paul visited him and cured him by praying and putting his hands on him. ⁹After this happened, the rest of the people on the island who had diseases also came and were cured. ¹⁰They bestowed many honors on us, and when we were about to sail, they put on board all the provisions we needed.

¹¹Three months later we set sail on a ship that had wintered at the island, an Alexandrian ship with the Twin Brothers as its figurehead. ¹²We put in at Syracuse and stayed there for three days; ¹³then we weighed anchor and came to Rhegium. After one day there a south wind sprang up, and on the second day we came to Puteoli. ¹⁴There we found believers and were invited to stay with them for seven days. And so we came to Rome. ¹⁵The believers from there, when they heard of us, came as far as the Forum of Appius and Three Taverns to meet us. On seeing them, Paul thanked God and took courage.

¹⁶When we came into Rome, Paul was allowed to live by himself, with the soldier who was guarding him.

The ship has run aground on Malta, an island south of Sicily. Here the passengers and crew wait out the winter storms before setting sail again for Italy. The Maltese natives are kind to the new arrivals and kindle a fire for their warmth. But as Paul is gathering brushwood for the fire, one of the sticks turns out to be a snake, which bites him as he nears the fire. The natives assume then that Paul must be guilty of murder. Although he has escaped a shipwreck, they believe, the justice of the gods will not allow him to live. But when Paul does not swell up or fall over dead, they change their opinion and hail him as a god. The power of the risen Christ continues to act through Paul. The incident with the snake is another way of demonstrating that Paul conquers the forces of evil wherever he goes. Jesus had told those whom he sends: "I have given you authority to tread on snakes and scorpions, and over all the power of the enemy; and nothing will hurt you" (Luke 10:19). Paul seems nonchalant about the incident, confident in God's promise that he will reach Rome.

The ship has come to land near the estate of the island's chief official, whose name is Publius. He welcomes the new arrivals and treats them hospitably for three days. The father of Publius is in bed with fever and dysentery, and when Paul prays over him and lays hands upon him, he is cured. As news of the healing spreads, the sick from throughout the island come to Paul and are cured. This summary of Paul's healings recalls similar summaries in the gospels of Jesus' cure of those who came to him. As Paul and the group of travelers set out again three months later, the thankful islanders express their gratitude by giving them gifts and all the supplies they need for their journey to Rome.

When the winter season has passed, the voyage resumes on another ship. It sails under the figurehead of Castor and Pollux, the twin sons of Zeus and protectors of those who sail the seas. The ship takes them first to Syracuse, the capital of Sicily, where they stay for three days. After this, they land at Rhegium, on the "toe" of Italy. After one day there, their sea voyage ends at Puteoli, an important harbor in the Bay of Naples. Here they find a group of Christians, who invite them to stay with them for seven days before the final leg of their journey on foot.

Luke's understated climax—"and so we came to Rome" (verse 14)—marks the completion of the travel narrative. A short journey by land from Puteoli takes them to the Via Appia, the well-known and well-worn road into the city of Rome. The Christians in the imperial city have received word of Paul's coming, and a number of them come out to meet the travelers. One group meets them at the Forum of Appius and the other nearer Rome at Three Taverns. Seeing these fellow Christians and knowing that they are living their faith openly in Rome motivates Paul and fills him with gratitude. When they reach the city from the south and the centurion reports his arrival, Paul is allowed to stay in private quarters under the guard of only one soldier. After a long and arduous journey, God's word to Paul is complete at the capital and hub of the empire.

Reflection and discussion

• Although Luke tells us that Paul healed many who came to him on the island of Malta, he does not tell us that Paul preached the gospel. Considering Paul's previous work in other places, would he have also preached the gospel and left behind a Christian community on Malta?

• When Paul was bitten by the snake, the natives of Malta said he was a murderer, and when he showed no adverse effects from the bite, they said he was a god. What do the natives need to learn about the ways of God?

•Paul was saved from the storm at sea, the shipwreck, and the snakebite. Why does Luke demonstrate that Paul was saved from the natural disasters?

• In what sense does Luke's phrase "and so we came to Rome" represent the climax and goal of the account of the early church told in Acts?

Prayer

Risen Lord, your apostle Paul sought to bear witness to you by all he said and did. Watch over me as I continue my life's journey, give me opportunities to evangelize, and bring me safely to the goal of your kingdom.

From morning until evening he explained the matter to them,
testifying to the kingdom of God and trying to convince them about Jesus
both from the law of Moses and from the prophets. Acts 28:23

Paul Proclaims
the Gospel in Rome

ACTS 28:17-31 *17Three days later he called together the local leaders of the Jews. When they had assembled, he said to them, "Brothers, though I had done nothing against our people or the customs of our ancestors, yet I was arrested in Jerusalem and handed over to the Romans. 18When they had examined me, the Romans wanted to release me, because there was no reason for the death penalty in my case. 19But when the Jews objected, I was compelled to appeal to the emperor—even though I had no charge to bring against my nation. 20For this reason therefore I have asked to see you and speak with you, since it is for the sake of the hope of Israel that I am bound with this chain." 21They replied, "We have received no letters from Judea about you, and none of the brothers coming here has reported or spoken anything evil about you. 22But we would like to hear from you what you think, for with regard to this sect we know that everywhere it is spoken against."*

²³After they had set a day to meet with him, they came to him at his lodgings in great numbers. From morning until evening he explained the matter to them, testifying to the kingdom of God and trying to convince them about Jesus both from the law of Moses and from the prophets. ²⁴Some were convinced by what he had said, while others refused to believe. ²⁵So they disagreed with each other; and as they were leaving, Paul made one further statement: "The Holy Spirit was right in saying to your ancestors through the prophet Isaiah,

²⁶'Go to this people and say,
You will indeed listen, but never understand,
and you will indeed look, but never perceive.
²⁷For this people's heart has grown dull,
and their ears are hard of hearing,
and they have shut their eyes;
so that they might not look with their eyes,
and listen with their ears,
and understand with their heart and turn—
and I would heal them.'

²⁸Let it be known to you then that this salvation of God has been sent to the Gentiles; they will listen."

³⁰He lived there two whole years at his own expense and welcomed all who came to him, ³¹proclaiming the kingdom of God and teaching about the Lord Jesus Christ with all boldness and without hindrance.

Luke's final scene describes Paul's proclamation of the gospel in Rome. He expresses Paul's ministry in Rome according to the same pattern he has followed throughout his travels. This outline of his proclamation is summarized in his Letter to the Romans: "For I am not ashamed of the gospel; it is the power of God for salvation to everyone who has faith, to the Jew first and also to the Greek" (Rom 1:16).

God's saving plan of salvation is available to everyone who opens their heart to what God has done in the Messiah. This message is the culmination of Israel's hope, so it is directed first of all to the Jews. But because it is intended for the whole world, Paul has directed his proclamation to the Gentiles scattered throughout the Greek-speaking world of the Roman Empire.

Within three days of his arrival, Paul gathers the Jewish leaders of Rome to speak to them about his situation. By calling them "brothers," he emphasizes his continuing unity with the Jewish community. Paul assures them that he has done nothing against his own people or their ancient traditions. The Jewish leaders of Jerusalem arrested him and turned him over to the Romans, who found no reason to put him to death.

Yet, because the religious leaders persisted to agitate over a period of two years, Paul declares that he had no choice but to appeal his case to the emperor. He announces to the leaders in Rome that what is truly at stake is "the hope of Israel" (verse 20). He is wearing a Roman chain, not for any disloyalty to his people, but for his loyalty to the hope that they all share.

After the Roman Jews express a desire to hear from Paul about the new Jewish sect that they have been hearing about, they meet with him in large numbers at his lodging (verse 23). He explains to them all day about Jesus the Messiah and the kingdom of God, basing his teachings on the Torah and prophets of Israel. The listeners disagree with one another; some believe and others refuse. And as they are departing, Paul reminds them of the warning that Isaiah had given to their ancestors (Isa 6:9-10). The eyes, ears, and hearts of God's people are closed and unresponsive to the new message of God (verses 26-27). They refuse to turn to God for their healing.

The book of Acts ends on a note of triumph. Paul declares, "This salvation of God has been sent to the Gentiles; they will listen." Although Paul is in chains, the gospel cannot be chained. Though first directed to the Jews, the good news of salvation is now sent to everyone. Even though Paul is still a prisoner, he lives under house arrest in his own rented lodgings with a guard, welcoming everyone who comes to him. Confidently and unhindered, Paul continues to preach about the kingdom of God and to teach about the Lord Jesus Christ (verses 30-31). His door is always open to anyone who will listen to him and consider his message.

Luke's conclusion demonstrates that God has fulfilled his plans: fulfilling the hope of Israel in Jesus and sharing that fulfillment with the world through Paul's witness "to the ends of the earth" (1:8). The gospel has been proclaimed from Jerusalem to Rome. Yet, the conclusion is not the end of the story of Christ's church. The church is still preaching and teaching the word of God to whoever will open their eyes, ears, and heart to the salvation God is offering to all.

Reflection and discussion

• How can closed eyes, ears, and hearts prevent people from experiencing God's salvation?

• What does Luke's last verse show about his central concern in writing this work?

•What is the most important way that this study of Acts has challenged me to act in the name of Jesus?

Prayer

Lord Jesus, hope of Israel and light to the Gentiles, continue to pour out your Spirit on the church so that we may continue the work of Peter and Paul. Let me bring your good news to everyone in need of your mercy and salvation.

SUGGESTIONS FOR FACILITATORS, GROUP SESSION 6

1. Welcome group members and make any final announcements or requests.

2. You may want to pray this prayer as a group:

Creating and Redeeming God, your apostle Paul found ways to serve you and to proclaim the gospel even in life's most difficult circumstances. Through calm waters and stormy seas, you assured him of your protective presence and promised him that he would reach his goal in Rome. Through the trials and sufferings of this life, calm our fears, give us strength, and make us confident in your promises. Show us ways to continue preaching and teaching the gospel through word, worship, and witness so that others may come to believe.

3. Ask one or more of the following questions:
   - How has this study of the Acts of the Apostles enriched your life?
   - In what way has this study challenged you the most?

4. Discuss lessons 25 through 30. Choose one or more of the questions for reflection and discussion from each lesson to discuss as a group.

5. Ask the group if they would like to study another in the Threshold Bible Study series. Discuss the topic and dates, and make a decision among those interested. Ask the group members to suggest people they would like to invite to participate in the next study series.

6. Ask the group to discuss the insights that stand out most from this study over the past six weeks.

7. Conclude by praying aloud the following prayer or another of your own choosing:

Holy Spirit of the living God, you inspired the writers of the Scriptures and you have guided our study during these weeks. Continue to deepen our love for the word of God in the holy Scriptures, and draw us more deeply into the heart of Jesus. We thank you for the confident hope you have placed within us and the gifts that build up the church. Through this study, lead us to worship and witness more fully and fervently, and bless us now and always with the fire of your love.

The
ACTS OF THE APOSTLES
in the Sunday Lectionary

ACTS 1:1-11
Ascension of the Lord
(58-ABC)

ACTS 1:12-14
7th Sunday of Easter
(59-A)

ACTS 1:15-17, 20A, 20C-26
7th Sunday of Easter
(60-B)

ACTS 2:1-11
Pentecost Sunday
(63-ABC)

ACTS 2:14, 22-33
3rd Sunday of Easter
(46-A)

ACTS 2:14A, 36-41
4th Sunday of Easter
(49-A)

ACTS 2:42-47
2nd Sunday of Easter
(43-A)

ACTS 3:13-15, 17-19
3rd Sunday of Easter
(47-B)

THE ACTS OF THE APOSTLES IN THE SUNDAY LECTIONARY

ACTS 4:8-12
4th Sunday of Easter
(50-B)

ACTS 4:32-35
2nd Sunday of Easter
(44-B)

ACTS 5:12-16
2nd Sunday of Easter
(45-C)

ACTS 5:27-32, 40B-41
3rd Sunday of Easter
(48-C)

ACTS 6:1-7
5th Sunday of Easter
(52-A)

ACTS 7:55-60
7th Sunday of Easter
(61-C)

ACTS 8:5-8, 14-17
6th Sunday of Easter
(55-A)

ACTS 9:26-31
5th Sunday of Easter
(53-B)

ACTS 10:25-26, 34-35, 44-48
6th Sunday of Easter
(56-B)

ACTS 10:34-38
Sunday after Epiphany: Baptism of the Lord
(21-ABC)

ACTS 10:34A, 37-43
Easter Sunday: Resurrection of the Lord
(42-ABC)

ACTS 13:14, 43-52
4th Sunday of Easter
(51-C)

ACTS 13:16-17, 22-25
Christmas: Vigil Mass
(13-ABC)

ACTS 14:21-27
5th Sunday of Easter
(54-C)

ACTS 15:1-2, 22-29
6th Sunday of Easter
(57-C)

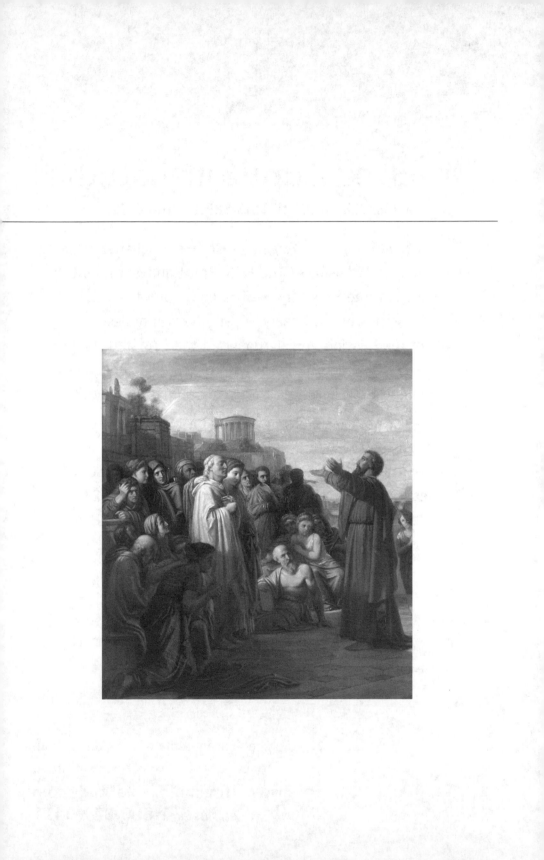

Ordering Additional Studies

TWENTY THIRD 23rd
PUBLICATIONS

To check availability or for a description
of each study, visit our website at
www.ThresholdBibleStudy.com
or call us at **1-800-321-0411**